THE LOVE LETTERS OF

William and Mary Wordsworth

William and Mary Wordsworth in their old age, by Margaret Gillies. The original, painted in 1839, was destroyed; this replica was made by the artist in 1859, after Mary's death. No portrait of Mary Wordsworth survives from her early or middle years. The Dove Cottage Trust, Grasmere.

THE LOVE LETTERS OF
William and Mary Wordsworth

EDITED BY
BETH DARLINGTON

Cornell University Press

ITHACA, NEW YORK

International Standard Book Number 0-8014-1261-7
Library of Congress Catalog Card Number 81-67177
Printed in the United States of America
*Librarians: Library of Congress cataloging information appears
on the last page of the book.*

For my parents

A blessed Marriage for him & for her it has been!

—Samuel Taylor Coleridge,
of the Wordsworths'
marriage, 1808

Preface

The love letters of William and Mary Wordsworth came to light in the spring of 1977 with a substantial body of other previously unknown documents of the Wordsworth family—the private papers of Mary Wordsworth and her youngest son, William—all up for auction at Sotheby's. The anonymous vendor proved later to be a stamp dealer in Carlisle, who claimed that he had bought the lot as scrap for a five-pound note; sorting it through for old postage stamps, he discovered his treasure. Here were manuscripts of poems, legal archives, and a vast cache of letters to and from the Wordsworth family. The most precious correspondence was the thirty-one letters written by the poet and his wife near the end of the first decade of their marriage. Mary apparently preserved and carefully protected these letters, following her husband's wish that they be "deposited side by side as a bequest for the survivor of us." After her death in 1859 at Rydal Mount, they must have passed with other written effects to William Wordsworth, Jr., then working and living in Carlisle. How the papers of Mary and her son were separated from other family papers—subsequently inherited by the younger William's son Gordon Graham Wordsworth and bequeathed by him to the Dove Cottage Trust in 1934—eludes explanation. Possibly they were squirreled away for nearly a century in a solicitor's office, but how they came to be discarded as scrap remains a tantalizing mystery. At Sotheby's sale, in July 1977, Cornell University purchased the new archive. When an export license was denied, the university sold the papers to the Trustees of Dove Cottage, and the papers now reside, appropriately, at the Wordsworth Library in Grasmere.

The new correspondence of William and Mary comprises fifteen letters written by the poet to his wife and sixteen written by her to him. Seven of the thirty-one letters date from the summer of 1810, nearly eight years after the Wordsworths' wedding. While Mary remained at home in Grasmere with their five children, the youngest not yet two months old, William journeyed to Leicestershire with his sister, Dorothy, to visit his patron, Sir George Beaumont, at Coleorton; thence he proceeded alone to Hindwell, in Wales, where he stayed with Mary's brother Thomas Hutchinson. The remaining twenty-four letters date from the spring of 1812 and document Wordsworth's sojourn in London, where he went to patch up a misunderstanding with Coleridge, while Mary visited her brother's farm in Wales.

Although William and Mary Wordsworth had been separated before during their marriage, these letters are the first they wrote for each other's eyes alone. Hitherto no letters written by Mary to William before 1837 were known to exist; few written by William to Mary before 1828 were known, and those (like the majority written after 1828) were of joint composition or multiply addressed, their tone more formal than tender. The new letters, however, provide an intimate and revealing picture of the early years of the Wordsworths' marriage.

The marriage metaphor is one of the great Romantic tropes, a symbol of wholeness achieved through difficult struggle and of redemption won after fragmentation and despair. Like Coleridge, Blake, and Shelley, Wordsworth drew on the metaphor in his poetry to embody the vision and shape the myth that gave meaning to his world. In the Prospectus to *The Recluse* he declared that his highest poetic purpose was to "chant . . . the spousal verse" of the *great* consummation: the wedding of the discerning human intellect to "this goodly universe / In love and holy passion." These letters show us the human experience out of which such a metaphor could be forged, the reality that lay behind the glory of the poet's dream.

The Wordsworths' correspondence pulsates not only with the steady rhythm of a deep mutual love and trust, but also with the elation of discovering the excitement of writing and receiving a passionate letter. Some readers may question the propriety of making such a personal correspondence public. Nearly a century ago Oscar Wilde emphatically expressed his contempt for such ventures in a sonnet, "On the Sale by Auction of Keats' Love Letters":

> These are the letters which Endymion wrote
> To one he loved in secret and apart,
> And now the brawlers of the auction-mart
> Bargain and bid for each tear-blotted note,
> Aye! for each separate pulse of passion quote
> The merchant's price! I think they love not art
> Who break the crystal of a poet's heart,
> That small and sickly eyes may glare or gloat.

In an era that feeds on the publication of intimate diaries and psychobiography, we might pause to recall Wilde's outrage and Wordsworth's own admonition against setting foot on nature's holiest places, probing to the heart, or murdering to dissect. Yet strong arguments press for publication. False images of William, Mary, and their marriage have gained currency in our time; these distortions need correction.

Editorial intrusion has been kept to a minimum in this volume. When the correspondents' intentions are obvious, omitted letters and words have been supplied in the transcriptions. Elsewhere the reader is invited to follow Wordsworth's own instruction to Mary: "excuse all blunders and fill up omissions by your own ingenuity." False starts, slips of the pen, and accidental repetitions of words or syllables have been silently corrected. The Wordsworths' spelling and punctuation have been preserved throughout. Empty brackets in the transcriptions indicate readings lost as a result of torn or badly worn spots in the manuscripts; frequently the wax seals destroyed a few phrases at the conclusions of letters. Letters and words within brackets are speculative readings when preceded by a question mark, otherwise material supplied editorially. Paragraphing has been introduced for the reader's convenience. The principle guiding annotation was to provide an informed context for the Wordsworths' thoughts and activities but to avoid freighting the letters with historical data.

In the preparation of this edition I have incurred numerous debts of gratitude. I owe special thanks to M. H. Abrams, Paul Betz, Brigid Boardman, James Butler, S. T. Chapman, Ruth Cohen, Hugh Crean, Jenny Dainty, Dan Davin, Simon Fenwick, Walter Garner, Jodi George, Stephen Gill, Karen Green, Carl Ketcham, George Kirkby, Peter Laver, Terry McCormick, Stephen Parrish, Mark Reed, John West, and Jonathan Wordsworth for advice and assistance; to the Trustees of Dove Cottage for their support and encouragement; to Vassar College for a research leave of absence and grants in aid; and to the National Endowment for the Humanities for a research fellowship.

BETH DARLINGTON

Poughkeepsie, New York

Contents

Contents

Illustrations

Maps

Abbreviations

DCP   Dove Cottage Papers, contained in the new collection at the Wordsworth Library, Dove Cottage, Grasmere

EY   *The Letters of William and Dorothy Wordsworth: The Early Years, 1787–1805,* ed. Ernest de Selincourt, 2d ed., rev. Chester L. Shaver (Oxford: Clarendon Press, 1967)

Jordan   John E. Jordan, *De Quincey to Wordsworth: A Biography of a Relationship, with the Letters of Thomas De Quincey to the Wordsworth Family* (Berkeley: University of California Press, 1962)

Masson   *The Collected Writings of Thomas De Quincey,* ed. David Masson, 14 vols. (Edinburgh: Adam & Charles Black, 1889–1890)

MY   *The Letters of William and Dorothy Wordsworth: The Middle Years, 1806–1820,* ed. Ernest de Selincourt, 2 vols., 2d ed.; Part I, 1806–1811, rev. Mary Moorman (Oxford: Clarendon Press, 1969); Part II, 1812–1820, rev. Mary Moorman and Alan G. Hill (Oxford: Clarendon Press, 1970)

THE LOVE LETTERS OF

William and Mary Wordsworth

Introduction

"In a Man's Letters, you know, Madam," Dr. Johnson explains to Mrs. Thrale, "his soul lies naked, his letters are only the mirrour of his breast, whatever passes within him is shown undisguised in its natural process. Nothing is inverted, nothing distorted, you see systems in their elements, you discover actions in their motives. . . . This is the pleasure of corresponding with a friend, where doubt and distrust have no place, and everything is said as it is thought. . . . These are the letters by which souls are united, and by which Minds naturally in unison move each other as they are moved themselves."[1] Ever eager for precise definition, Dr. Johnson here attempts to clarify his notion of "the great epistolick art." Again, we must give that wise old lexicographer the palm. In these few thoughtful lines he brushes aside innumerable pretentious disquisitions on the subject to remind us why letters matter and what good letters genuinely are. He speaks here of letters of friendship rather than letters of love, but that distinction blurs nearly into insignificance when we realize that letters of friendship at their best are love letters—must be so to unite two spirits as Johnson describes. Similarly the finest love letters are more than mere billets doux, more than concentrated effusions of passion. They, too, must mirror all that passes within the mind and heart, so that in their leaves a whole soul is laid open, a whole life re-

[1] 27 October 1777. *The Letters of Samuel Johnson*, ed. R. W. Chapman, 3 vols. (Oxford: Clarendon Press, 1952), II, 228.

vealed. The love letters of William and Mary Wordsworth do
this. More than any biographical documents known hitherto,
these new letters show us, without distortion, who William and
Mary Wordsworth were and what sort of love bound them so
compellingly together as man and wife.

Epicures whose taste for love letters was stimulated by Antonia Fraser's anthology of sighs, tears, swellings of the bosom,
and delicious melting transports may be disappointed.[2] Wordsworth offers no sizzling rhetoric to match Napoleon's sensa-
tional gallantries to Josephine: "I hope to hold you in my arms
before long, when I shall lavish upon you a million kisses,
burning as the equatorial sun." Nor does the poet strike the
pyrotechnic chords of Liszt improvising a two-part invention
with Marie d'Agoult: "Oh! Leave me free to rave in my de-
lirium. Drab, tame, constricting reality is no longer enough for
me. We must live our lives to the full, loving and suffering to
extremes!" And so on. "That am not I," the Wife of Bath ex-
claims in repudiating a way of life antithetic to her character,
and this is not Wordsworth. The Wordsworths' love letters are
not flamboyantly self-dramatizing, nor is their burden love
alone. Like the Lyrical Ballads, they chronicle "incidents and
situations from common life, and . . . relate or describe them
. . . in [the] language really used by men." Like the Lyrical Ballads, too, they create their own world, into which we are gently
led, where feeling gives importance to action and situation.

The love of Mary Hutchinson and William Wordsworth was
rooted in childhood. Mary was only a few months younger
than William, and like the Wordsworth children was orphaned
at an early age. She grew up in Penrith, and there, while still a
child, he visited his maternal grandparents and attended school
with her. Later, during his vacations from Hawkshead Gram-
mar School and Cambridge, Wordsworth came to know Mary
well, and to her he "breathed [his] first fond vows." In *The
Prelude* he speaks of their roaming over the hills together at
seventeen as "the blessed time of early love." At twenty-one,

[2]*Love Letters: An Anthology*, ed. Antonia Fraser (Harmondsworth: Penguin,
1977). The letters quoted appear on pp. 192 and 67.

however, in France, Wordsworth fell in love with Annette Vallon. Swept away by his political faith in the French Revolution—

> Bliss was it in that dawn to be alive,
> But to be young was very heaven!

—and conceivably by his first experiences of passionate love, he seems temporarily to have forgotten his calmer English commitments. There can be no doubt that when he left France at the end of 1792 Wordsworth intended to find a job, marry Annette, and bring her and their daughter Caroline to England. As it happened, however, the wars in France separated them for ten years. The tones of Annette's two surviving letters of 1793 are full of hope and affection: "Come, my love, my husband. Receive the tender embraces of your wife, of your daughter. . . . I love you forever."[3] But when they finally met during the Peace of Amiens in 1802, William was engaged to Mary Hutchinson, and Annette, as far as we know, had accepted the fact that marriage to him was no longer possible.

At some point during the years of uncertainty about his future with Annette, Mary had slipped quietly back into William's life. In 1796–97 she spent six months with him and Dorothy at Racedown, in Dorset.[4] Perhaps they did not yet acknowledge a renewal of love; but looking back in 1810, the poet felt that had he accompanied Mary on her journey when she left, they would surely have done so:

> You would have walked on Northwards with me at your side, till unable to part from each other we might have come in sight of those hills which skirt the road for so many miles, and thus continuing our journey . . . we should have seen so deeply into each

[3] 20 March 1793; my translation. A copy of the original letter is printed in Emile Legouis's *William Wordsworth and Annette Vallon* (London: J. M. Dent, 1922), pp. 125–27.

[4] Coleridge's friendship and Dorothy's affection are usually credited with rousing Wordsworth from depression in 1797 and inspiring him to begin to compose the works of his great decade of poetic creativity. It is possible, however, that William's reawakened love for Mary played a more influential role in this transition than has commonly been supposed.

others hearts, and been so fondly locked in each others arms, that
we should have braved the worst and parted no more.

William and Mary did not decide in 1797 to "brave the worst"
(presumably to face opposition from their families and to marry without money), but their long visits to each other's homes
during the next five years are evidence of their reluctance to
be parted. Within two months of the time William and Dorothy set up house at Dove Cottage, in December 1799, he had
fetched Mary over for her first visit, and by the end of 1801 they
had decided to marry. "There never lived on earth a better
woman than Mary H.," Dorothy asserted, "and I have not a
doubt but that she is in every respect formed to make an excellent wife to my Brother."[5] The wedding took place on 4 October
1802 at Brompton, in Yorkshire, and Mary became at last a
member of the household in which she had so often been a
visitor.

Regrettably, no contemporary letters or journals record William's and Mary's feelings as they began their married life. In
the absence of such evidence, the relationship has often been
misconstrued. Because of his closeness to Dorothy over the
preceding seven years—the inspiration for some of his most
beautiful poetry—and because her journal entries, especially on
his wedding day, expose an attachment more demonstrative
emotionally than is common between sister and brother, readers have frequently assumed that Wordsworth's marriage was
one of convenience, that his physical passion had been ex-
pended on Annette and his spiritual passion on Dorothy.
Wrongly, some people have even judged the marriage a "desperate remedy," a "reluctant rejection" of an incestuous
union.[6] If William did indeed love Mary as passionately before

---

[5]*EY*, p. 377.
[6]F. W. Bateson, *Wordsworth: A Reinterpretation*, 2d ed. (London: Longmans,
1956), pp. 156–57. For the most sensible discussion of Wordsworth's relationship with his sister, see Mary Moorman's "William and Dorothy Wordsworth," the Katja Reissner Lecture, 1970, in *Essays by Divers Hands: Transactions
of the Royal Society of Literature*, n.s. 37 (London: Oxford University Press, 1972),
pp. 75–94.

their marriage as the correspondence of 1810 and 1812 attests, why, we might ask, did he write no love letters to her then? Thomas De Quincey offers one explanation when he argues that the postures of conventional courtship were quite simply contrary to Wordsworth's nature:

> To us who, in after years, were Wordsworth's friends, or, at least, intimate acquaintances . . . the most interesting circumstance in this marriage, the one which perplexed us exceedingly, was the very possibility that it should ever have been brought to bear. For we could not conceive of Wordsworth as submitting his faculties to the humilities and devotion of courtship. That self-surrender— that prostration of mind by which a man is too happy and proud to express the profundity of his service to the woman of his heart—it seemed a mere impossibility that ever Wordsworth should be brought to feel for a single instant; and what he did not sincerely feel, assuredly he was not the person to profess. . . . never could he, in any emphatic sense, have been a lover.[7]

One could also cite a certain reticence in Wordsworth about his deepest emotions, or speculate that decorum and integrity must have inhibited him in the early years. His obligations to Annette and Caroline were unresolved, and despite his obvious interest in children and thoughts about parenthood, he couldn't really afford a family of his own.[8] A further silencing factor may have been Wordsworth's nerves. Writing upset him. Even talking about intellectual topics on which he held strong convictions led to illness and sleeplessness. Precious visits and the tireless correspondence carried on primarily by Dorothy and Mary were made to suffice—during courtship.[9] Ten years later the man who grumbled that he always disliked writing letters avowed that he "could write on till the end of time" to Mary and that he was "never so happy" during their separa-

---

[7]Masson, II, 283–84.

[8]Wordsworth's financial situation was insecure until 1803, when a debt owed to his father at his death twenty years earlier was finally discharged.

[9]Although the Wordsworths were savers, most of these letters have not survived. It is possible that Mary destroyed them after William's death, but the conjecture cannot be substantiated.

tions as when writing to her. Indeed, his final words in this correspondence are "How gladly could I scribble away."

All too often Mary Wordsworth has been dismissed as a dull and bland *Hausfrau* who played little part in the poet's inner life. This she was not. Wordsworth's poems, a verbal sketch by De Quincey, and finally Mary's own letters disclose a far more animated image. In *The Prelude* Wordsworth remarks on her sweetness, gentleness, and lack of affectation, but his finest literary tribute is the exquisite lyric "She was a Phantom of delight." There Mary is honored as

> A perfect Woman, nobly planned,
> To warn, to comfort, and command;
> And yet a Spirit still, and bright
> With something of angelic light.

In 1807 De Quincey found in Mary "a sunny benignity—a radiant graciousness—such as in this world I never saw surpassed."[10] More than her previously published letters, Mary's love letters attest the frankness, strength, and depth of her character. They declare her admiration—indeed, near worship—of her husband and her pleasure in her role as wife and mother, but also her refined sensibility, ready humor, and good sense.

Mary can be practical and prosaic: "At Liverpool you must order for us a Cask of rice & another of oil," she instructs William. "Do not neglect this & enquire of Mr Crump about that money which he collected for the Green's." On occasion she can be scaldingly sarcastic: "I doubt indeed Mr W[ilson] will marry Miss Jane . . . her countenance belies her if her mind is not made of lard." But most often we are touched by the scope of Mary's loving concern, her generous sympathy of spirit— here, for example, when she has just read of the straitened circumstances of William's French family:

[10]Masson, II, 238.

Dear Caroline & Annette I cannot help recurring to them again
the account they give of themselves is very affecting— & creditable to the Mother— She [Caroline] must be a nice Girl. . . . God
bless her I should love her dearly & divide my last with her were
it needful— God bless them both & thee my best beloved my soul
& every nerve is full of thee.

When Mary confides her love to her husband, readers may de-
tect a bashful modesty, but here, too, her letters serve as a
faithful "mirrour of h[er] breast." She emerges from these
pages, at last, in full stature, a woman worthy of De Quincey's
estimate, a "second self of the poet."[11]

Written to the edge in his small, cramped hand, Wordsworth's letters similarly deepen our knowledge of his character; here, also, "his soul lies naked." The familiar features are
present: we recognize his fervent absorption in politics and his
captious fulminations against the literary productions of his
contemporaries; his eye for natural beauty and his ability to see
human dignity in a poignant though commonplace incident;
his enthusiasm for travel in new places; his concern for his children; his repeated complaints of ill health; and his somber
brooding on the transience of human life. But the chime of a
new note sounds as Wordsworth the lover eloquently confesses
his passion to Mary:

I love thee so deeply and tenderly and constantly, and with such
perfect satisfaction delight & happiness to my soul, that I scarcely
can bring my pen to write of any thing else. — How blest was I to
hear of those sweet thoughts of me which had flowed along thy
dreams; sleeping & waking my Love let me be with thee as thou
art with me!

He demands more letters from Mary—"intensely connubial"
letters—and rails petulantly if they fail to arrive promptly.
When Mary discloses that his letters have overwhelmed her
with surprise and pleasure, he exults in her response: "O my
blessing, how happy was I in learning that my Letter had

[11]Masson, II, 237.

moved thee so deeply, and thy delight in reading had if possible been more exquisite than mine in writing."

"Wordsworth is by nature incapable of being in Love, tho' no man more tenderly attached," Coleridge asserted to Henry Crabb Robinson in 1811; "hence he ridicules the existence of any other passion, than a compound of Lust with Esteem & Friendship, confined to one Object, first by accidents of Association, and permanently, by the force of Habit & a sense of Duty."[12] Coleridge's statement, written during a period of painful and bitter alienation from Wordsworth, may well distort Wordsworth's meaning in some earlier conversation; after all, in 1808 he had termed the marriage "blessed" for both William and Mary. But beyond that, Coleridge appears to debar Wordsworth from the freemasonry of lovers for failure "by nature" to comprehend and value the transcendent power of spiritual love. William's letters to Mary bear witness in his defense. To be sure, sexual passion did fire his love for his wife, but not as lust crudely compounded with esteem and friendship. Here physical and spiritual passion commingle and fuse. "Every hour of absence now is a grievous loss," William avows, "because we have been parted sufficiently to feel how profoundly in soul & body we love each other; and to be taught what a sublime treasure we possess in each others love."

In the same letter to Crabb Robinson quoted earlier, Coleridge proposes, "True human Love [is] two hearts, like two correspondent concave mirrors, having a common focus, while each reflects and magnifies the other, and in the other itself, is an endless reduplication, by sweet Thoughts & Sympathies." The Wordsworths' letters shine with that reflection, that "endless reduplication," as William and Mary alternately vow that they are the most blessed of human creatures and protest that their hearts beat with one pulse. "Oh William," Mary avers, "I can not tell thee how I love thee, & thou must not desire it— but feel it, O feel it in the fullness of thy soul & *believe* that

[12] 12 March 1811. *Collected Letters of Samuel Taylor Coleridge*, ed. Earl Leslie Griggs, 6 vols. (Oxford: Clarendon Press, 1956–71), III, 305.

I am the happiest of Wives & of Mothers & of all Women the most blessed."

William, too, beseeches Mary to look into her own heart when pen and paper—mere letters—finally seem inadequate to convey his feelings:

Oh my beloved—but I ought not to trust myself to this senseless & visible sheet of paper; speak for me to thyself, find the evidence of what is passing within me in *thy* heart, in thy mind, in thy steps as they touch the green grass, in thy limbs as they are stretched upon the soft earth; in thy own involuntary sighs & ejaculations, in the trembling of thy hands, in the tottering of thy knees, in the blessings which thy lips pronounce, find it in thy lips themselves, & such kisses as I often give to the empty air, and in the aching of thy bosom, and let a voice speak for me in every thing within thee & without thee.

These are indeed "letters by which souls are united." They portray a vital relationship, refined and tempered by nearly ten years of closely shared experience—a marriage of true and like minds. The poet's own words distill for us the very essence of such a union: "Every day every hour every moment makes me feel more deeply how blessed we are in each other, how purely how faithfully how ardently, and how tenderly we love each other; I put this last word last because, though I am persuaded that a deep affection is not uncommon in married life, yet I am confident that a lively, gushing, thought-employing, spirit-stirring, passion of love, is very rare even among good people." He was, of course, right.

Abbreviated genealogy

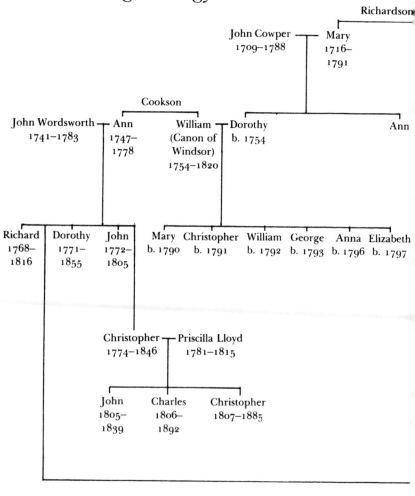

Richardson

John Cowper — Mary
1709–1788   1716–
             1791

Cookson

John Wordsworth — Ann   William — Dorothy   Ann
1741–1783   1747–   (Canon of   b. 1754
                 1778   Windsor)
                          1754–1820

Richard | Dorothy | John   Mary   Christopher William   George   Anna   Elizabeth
1768– | 1771– | 1772–   b. 1790   b. 1791   b. 1792   b. 1793   b. 1796   b. 1797
1816 | 1855 | 1805

Christopher — Priscilla Lloyd
1774–1846   1781–1815

John   Charles   Christopher
1805–   1806–   1807–1885
1839   1892

John   Dorothy
1803–   (Dora)
1875   1804–
           1847

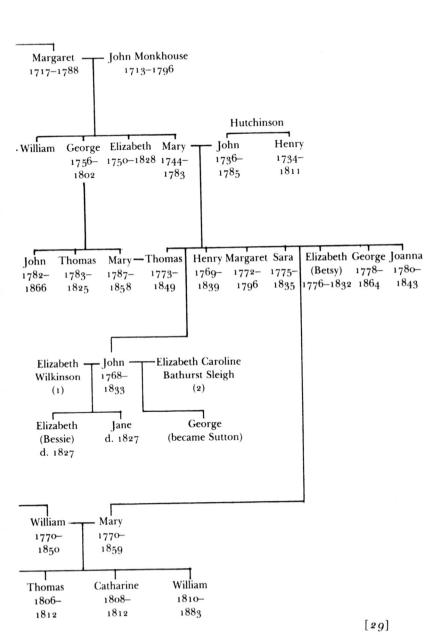

Margaret ——— John Monkhouse
1717–1788   1713–1796

Hutchinson

. William George Elizabeth Mary ——— John   Henry
          1756–   1750–1828 1744–   1736–   1734–
          1802   1783   1785   1811

John   Thomas Mary—Thomas Henry Margaret Sara   Elizabeth   George Joanna
1782–   1783–   1787– 1773– 1769– 1772–   1775–   (Betsy)   1778–   1780–
1866   1825   1858   1849   1839   1796   1835   1776–1832   1864   1843

Elizabeth ——— John ———Elizabeth Caroline
Wilkinson   1768–   Bathurst Sleigh
   (1)   1833   (2)

Elizabeth   Jane   George
(Bessie)   d. 1827   (became Sutton)
d. 1827

William ——— Mary
1770–   1770–
1850   1859

Thomas   Catharine   William
1806–   1808–   1810–
1812   1812   1883

[29]

The Letters

1

William to Mary, 22 July 1810

William Wordsworth, Jr., the youngest of the Wordsworths' children, was born at Allan Bank in Grasmere on 12 May 1810. He arrived, in his aunt Dorothy's words, "stout and healthy with the Wordsworth nose" (*MY*, I, 410). Six weeks later William and Dorothy set off to visit Sir George Beaumont's home, Coleorton, near Ashby de la Zouch in Leicestershire. They departed about 29 June and proceeded at a leisurely pace, by coach, chaise, and on foot, stopping to visit friends and see the sights along their way. Beaumont was an amateur artist, a collector, and a patron of Wordsworth. Seven years earlier he had given the poet a piece of land, and had hospitably housed the Wordsworth family at the hall farm at Coleorton in the winter of 1806–7, when Dove Cottage seemed too cramped for their growing numbers.

Although the visitors were mistaken for wandering troopers on their arrival, they were soon welcomed warmly and obviously enjoyed their sojourn. William's thoughts bent homeward, however, to Mary and their children. There were five: John, seven; Dorothy (often called Dora to distinguish her from her aunt), nearly six; Thomas, four; Catharine, twenty-two months; and Baby William. Wordsworth fretted about the health of each, but expressed special concern for Catharine; in April, after eating a quantity of raw carrot, she had suffered a mild stroke, which left her lame and vulnerably weak.

Sara Hutchinson, Mary's younger sister, was staying with her brother Tom on his farm in Wales; William intended to visit them after his holiday with the Beaumonts. Sara Fricker Coleridge, wife of Samuel Taylor Coleridge, lived with their children in Keswick. Charles Lloyd was a Birmingham banker and the father of the Wordsworths' neighbor Charles Lloyd, Jr., a poet, and of Priscilla

Lloyd Wordsworth, wife of William's younger brother Christopher. Alexander Blair, a literary friend from Birmingham, had come to Coleorton with William and Dorothy but did not remain long. John Gregory Crump of Liverpool was the Wordsworths' landlord at Allan Bank. The Reverend Joseph Wilkinson, another amateur artist, published *Select Views in Cumberland, Westmoreland and Lancashire* in 1810, for which Wordsworth had agreed to write the accompanying descriptive text. The work became a tedious chore for the poet—he was little impressed with Wilkinson's skill—and to spare him drudgery, Dorothy helped him to complete the project.

William's allusions to Middleham and Gallow Hill harked back to the days before his marriage. Mary's brother George then farmed at Bishop Middleham, near Durham, and Tom at Gallow Hill, near Brompton, in east Yorkshire. Mary had kept house for Tom, but also stayed with George for extended periods, and William had visited her at both places.

William complained frequently of inflammation of the eyelids (probably trachoma), from which he had first suffered in 1805. It plagued him for the rest of his life, often making writing and reading extremely painful and requiring him to shade his eyes from bright lights.

Sunday Morning

D—[1] is gone to church at Ashby with the ladies, and I seize with eagerness this opportunity to write to my dearest Love. —You will guess that I have been much agitated by your late letters, and the account of the vexations you have under gone; above all I was so much affected by the manner in which you spoke of dear little Catharine and her lameness; that I had great difficulty in preventing myself from setting off immediately to see you both, and to be assured that she was not so lame as my Imagination pictured to me. The other vexation I

[1] Dorothy Wordsworth.

hope will be soon over, as there is nothing formidable in the complaint if taken in time. When I recollect, however, what Thomas suffered from the hooping-cough I can not but have many alarms for little W^m. and I do earnestly wish that it might please God to preserve him from that complaint till the time of teething was past. — We travelled from Manchester with a little Babe, in the hooping Cough, and it was quite grievous to see how much it had been reduced and what it suffered. — Your good sense would enable you to tolerate the ill conduct of the servants; which, I confess, is very mortifying; but if one reflects, nothing different can be expected from persons so educated. To Mrs C—[2] such conduct would have been insupportable. Fail not to remember what was desired about your mouth, as I do earnestly pray that you may be relieved from that uncomfortable feeling, which at the same time can not but be injurious to your health. — And I am confident that it is a complaint within the reach of medicine: —

We have now been here a fortnight and every thing has been done which kindness could do to make us happy; and certainly we have enjoyed ourselves much especially D—. who is grown very fat and looks better than she has done, since she had that complaint at Racedown: Her throat and neck are quite filled up; and if it were not for her teeth she would really look quite young. I never saw a more rapid and striking improvement in the health and appearance of any one. She has a most excellent appetite, as good a digestion and is never tired. For my own part though I should feel it a disgrace to be discont[ent]ed to any oppressive degree, with so much affectionateness, & tranquil and innocent pleasure about me, yet I do feel, that to no place where I am stationary some time can I ever be perfectly reconciled, even for a short time. When I am moving about I am not so strongly reminded of my home, and you and our little ones and the places which I love. Therefore I must say though not without regret do I say it, that I cannot help being anxious that I were gone, as when I move I shall feel myself moving towards you; though by a long circuit. O my beloved

[2]Sara Coleridge.

how my heart swells at the thought; and how dearly should I have enjoyed being alone with you so long! — But I must go hence into Wales; surely, sweet love, this is very unlucky. Nor could I reconcile myself to it, did I not think that you regretted the necessity as much as I do. — This journey will be the greatest proof of my regard to your Sister Sara[3] that it has ever been in my power to give her, or perhaps ever will be; and I should not be sorry that she could to a certain degree feel it as such; I say, to a degree for thoroughly to comprehend the extent and depth of the sacrifice is utterly impossible. S— has a tender heart and a loving spirit, but she is neither a wife nor a mother; nor can know any thing how I have longed to be with you— as I might be now. — Do not think, Darling, that I repine, no, I have much pleasure in making this sacrifice both for her sake and yours— You often laugh at me about Duty, but this [is] a pure march of duty, at vast expence of inclination if ever one was made by man. —

But I will leave this subject to say a word about our manner of spending our time. We are down to breakfast between half past eight and nine; from eleven to half past two I mostly ride with Sir G—.[4] at three we dine: between six and seven have tea, and walk till nine; once or twice we have had a little reading in the afternoon. There are several pleasant walks about this place, most if not all of which we have been together; but, of course this is a country that is much improved by summer. Yesterday evening we peeped into a cottage where sate, by a shining fire, an old blind Man, one of the tenants. D— asked him if [he] had had much pain when he lost his sight— he replied, "no, that it declined gradually away as the sun goes down at night: a very beautiful expression! Many of the Cottages are very neat and the gardens of almost all are well tended: we entered another beside which stood a sycamore tree, the age of which the man begged me to guess— it was six & thirty years old, and had been planted by himself; of course it takes up a great space of his little garden, but he said, "he

[3]Sara Hutchinson.
[4]Sir George Beaumont.

William Wordsworth, by Benjamin Robert Haydon, 1818. Drawn for Mary Wordsworth, the portrait was dubbed the Brigand and hung in the dining room at Rydal Mount until her death. The National Portrait Gallery, London.

would not part with his tree on any account; he was fond of trees and it sheltered his house". This man was getting into years and a Widower; he had [a] daughter in the house with him the rest of his family (six in number) were gotten from him: this daughter was eighteen, and he said "My Wife died of her." I dont know whether the expression be common but it struck me as a moving one; and I blessed God inwardly at the thought how often you had passed safely through that danger, and were still a flourishing mother. Indeed I am never instructed, never delighted, never touchd by a tender feeling but my heart instinctively turns to you. I never see a flower that pleases me but I wish for you. —

How happy should I be could I make this letter more dear and acceptable to you by giving you good news about my eye; but really it has made no progress these ten days. Nor is it any worse. The inflammation is certainly much less, than it once was; but it is still very large; though attended with no pain. I am sure it is retarded by the cause I mentioned, for which I never suffered half so much as during this absence from you, which I attribute in a great degree to our long previous separation; which really has left me nearly in the same state as I was when you were at Middleham and Gallow hill; with a thousand tender thoughts intermingled, and consciousnesses of realized bliss and happiness, to render separation from you heavier and more uneasy. Our Friends here look forward to a repetition of this visit next year; but I cannot think of any thing of the kind; nor will I ever, except from a principle of duty, part from you again, to stay any where more than one week. I cannot bear it. I feel the shortness and uncertainty of life; I feel that we must separate finally so soon, even if our lives be lengthened, that it seems criminal to me in a high degree, to part from you except from a strong call of unquestionable moral obligation. —

Where are you now; certainly, I think, not a[t] Church— — It wants 20 minutes of twelve— you are not sewing; for it is Sunday; the Children, are perhaps at Church, as I hope you have been able to keep them clear from the contagion. And yet it would perhaps be unseemly to send them to a place of public resort till the house was rid of the complaint— What then can you be all doing? strange that I should be at a loss, and yet I am; are you sitting in the front room? or strolling in the garden? I can not answer this question to my satisfaction— never mind— I can see your faces one by one, above all yours, my joy, my repose, my hope, and my support in every good thought or profitable feeling that enters into my spirit: —

How can I contrive the sooner to receive a Letter from you, in [   ] may pour out your heart & soul to me? should I say direct to me [   ] post office Birmingham or Ludlow, but I am not sure that I [   ] by Ludlow, and a Letter directed to Birmingham might possibly be carried to Lloyds. If I had heard from Mr Blair, I should request you to direct to me at his house; but he must have written and his letter is miscarried. However if I do hear from [him] in time; I shall request that you will write to me at his house; and again that I may have another Letter from you immediately on my arrival in Wales; a Letter for myself and of which I need only read parts to the rest of the family— I know that S—[5] will take no offense at this; for my soul demands such Letters, they seem to unite me to you person & spirit body and soul, in the privacy of sacred retirement, spite of the distance that separates us. O Dear & honoured Woman how blessed has been my lot! and how could I either long to live or lay down my life for thee even as it should please God to appoint! — But I must turn from these awful thoughts, to things external, and more fit to be trusted to this frail paper. — —

At the utmost I shall only stay here a fortnight more, I hope not more than eleven or twelve days; but I have not heard from Sara, and I do not like the thought (for my health's sake) of walking thirty or forty miles at the end of my journey; after a fortnight in Wales I hope to set my face towards home, oh with what joy. In the mean time write to me not less than twice a week on any account; and as soon as I leave this place I shall write to thee my love at least as often; so take care to have people sent over to the office— By the by let somebody be employed in cleaning the quick-set Hedge for Mr Crump— I fore-

[5]Sara Hutchinson.

Sir George Beaumont, by J. Wright, copied from a portrait by John Hoppner painted in 1806. Wright's watercolor was owned by Lord Mulgrave. The National Portrait Gallery, London.

Lady Beaumont, copied from a portrait by Sir Joshua Reynolds, 1778.
Later portraits of Lady Beaumont do not appear to have survived.
The Dove Cottage Trust, Grasmere.

see we shall have much trouble about the parsonage—. I must not forget to tell thee that Sir G— has made me a present of a small & neat watch (a gold one I believe) but what is of more consequence he says it goes very well. This will be to me a great accommodation, and I shall wear it with much pleasure for the givers sake. I have read nothing at all since I came here, nor had any inclination to read; but I am somewhat grieved that my eye has benefited so little by this long holiday. D— has been so good as to abridge the sheets I wrote for Wilkinson for my own part I have no longer any interest in the thing; so he must make what he can of them; as I can not do the thing in my own way I shall merely task myself with getting through it with the least trouble.

I must now prepare to bid you farewell— kiss all the children for me, and remember me to the servants. I hope you will have no visitors to disturb you; and that you will get through the hay and your other troubles and hindrances speedily, and without injury. Kiss little Catharine for me ten times over, and little William in the loneliness and peace of the night for his dear Fathers sake; and above all things take care of your own precious health. I could write on till the end of time but I must yield to the necessities of things. How do I long to tread for the first time the road that will bring me in sight of Grasmere, to pant up the hill of Allan bank to cross the threshold to see to touc[h] you to speak to you & hear you spea[k] [ta]ke care— farewell

Fail not to write to me with out reserve; never have I been able to receive such a Letter from you, let me not then be disappointed, but give me your heart that I may kiss the words a thousand times! —

I must bid you again farewell with a thousand kisses, on this side the paper.   W.W   x x

2

Mary to William, 1–3 August 1810

Mary penned her reply to William in moments snatched between household chores. Her letter flashes an almost dizzying
kaleidoscope of local and family names and news. Fanny Turner
and Sarah Youdell, the two servant girls, darting in and out, and
children running, creeping, and calling form the steadier frame of
the shifting pattern.

A new curate had arrived, the Reverend William Johnson, who
later became a good family friend and acquired the affectionate
nickname Johnsy. He had walked into a Trollopian situation. The
old curate, the Reverend Edward Rowlandson, was retiring after
having served the parish for half a century, but the responsibilities
of his successor were not yet defined. Young Johnson hoped to
preach in the village church and teach in the village school, but
Gawen Mackereth, a Grasmere native nearly sixty-five years old,
had filled the post of schoolmaster and appeared reluctant to sur-
render it. The parish rector, the Reverend Thomas Jackson, who
lived in Langdale, obviously wished to avoid entanglement in the
conflict. Johnson asked Mary about a poem on the death of
Charles Gough, a Manchester artist who died in a fall on Helvellyn; on this mountain near Grasmere his dog kept watch by his
body until climbers discovered it three months later. Wordsworth
learned of the incident in 1805 and composed the poem *Fidelity*,
published in *Poems, in Two Volumes* (1807). Walter Scott's *Helvellyn*
(1805) treats the same subject.

Robert Newton kept the village inn at Church Stile, opposite the
churchyard in Grasmere. John Green, a local butcher and cattle
dealer, lived at Pavement End. Peggy Ashburner and her husband, Thomas, a crofter, dwelt at Town End in Grasmere, across
the road from Dove Cottage. Mary Dawson had been the Words-

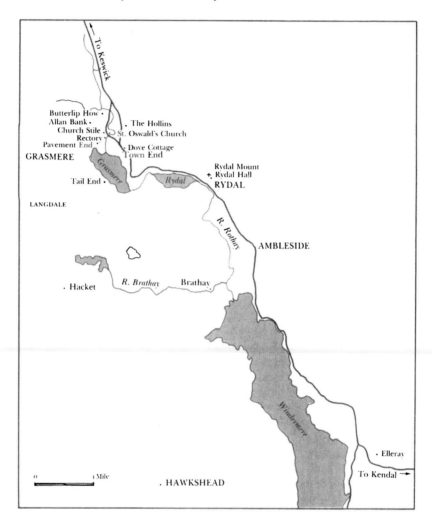

worths' servant at Dove Cottage, later cook for the Lloyds at Brathay, and then housekeeper for the author Thomas De Quincey (Mary calls him Quince or Q.), who leased Dove Cottage in 1809. Margaret Sym Wilson was the mother of John Wilson, an enthusiastic sportsman and man of letters who lived at Elleray, in Windermere. When his fortune turned and he was obliged to earn his livelihood, Wilson achieved fame as Christopher North in his reviews for *Blackwood's Magazine* and later was appointed Professor of Moral Philosophy at the University of Edinburgh. Wilson and De Quincey were the godfathers of little Willy Wordsworth. The Astleys, sporting friends of Wilson, disturbed the tranquillity of Grasmere with their loud harum-scarum behavior. Earlier Mary had alluded to their presence in the valley as an "infest[ation] by a horde of the Astley tribe" (*MY,* I, 430). One of the Astleys from the vicinity of Manchester rented Tail (or Dale) End, on the southwest side of Grasmere; his brother-in-law established himself at Robert Newton's inn. Jane Green worked for the Wordsworths as temporary domestic help in the summer of 1810.

Jane Pollard Marshall had been a close girlhood friend of Dorothy Wordsworth and later of the whole family; she was married to John Marshall, a linen manufacturer, and lived near Leeds. Tommy's zest for hoarding string was preceded by a craze for playing with pots and pans, which had won him the pet name Potiphar.

Mary sent her letter to Hindwell, her brother Tom's farm, in Radnorshire. She forgot, momentarily, that she was writing to her husband rather than her sister Sara as she commented on a letter from her oldest brother, Jack (or John) Hutchinson, who farmed at Stockton, in Yorkshire. The family crisis that had boiled up is not entirely clear, but the problem centered around the care of her sister Betsy Hutchinson, who was slightly feebleminded and required special attendance. Mrs. H. was John's second wife, Elizabeth Caroline Bathurst Sleigh Hutchinson. I have not been able to identify Judy and Nancy. Mary hoped that Betsy might make a home with Miss Sarah Weir, an old friend of the Hutchinsons; Dora Wordsworth later attended Miss Weir's small school for girls at Appleby.

Grasmere Aug. 1st— Wednesday Mor[g]—
O My William!

it is not in my power to tell thee how I have been affected by
this dearest of all letters— it was so unexpected— so new a
thing to see the breathing of thy inmost heart upon paper that
I was quite overpowered, & now that I sit down to answer thee
in the loneliness & depth of that love which unites us & which
cannot be felt but by ourselves, I am so agitated & my eyes are
so bedimmed that I scarcely know how to proceed— I have
brought my paper, after having laid my baby upon thy sacred
pillow, into my own, into THY own room— & write from Sara's
little Table, retired from the window which looks upon the
lasses strewing out the hay to an uncertain Sun. —

I was intending to say now that I had shut myself up here to
be out of the way of interruption, when I heard D. leading C.[1]
upstairs in search of me— I am followed by them into every
corner— I led them back & before I had put C. out of my
Arms I was summoned to the door. it was the New Curate who
rang. I met with him last night, at Ro[bt] Newton's where I had
occasion to call in my way to the Town-end, & lucky it was for
me that I did so, for if I had not been detained a short while
there, I should have been at home again before John Green
returned from Ambleside & brought me my treasure which in
that case I might not yet have received. This poor Man fears a
disappointment, for Gowan[2] I suppose has been possessed that
he need not give up the School unless he chuses— & he keeps
his Chair— Mr Jackson is too busy to interfere, & I know not
that he has the power to turn him— G— out— so this poor
Man is uncertain whether he is to be schoolmaster or no— he
says he will not contend for it, particularly with an old man—
but he thinks that if the Town would appoint him he would in
time give satisfaction— he seems to aspire to raise the School to

[1]Dora and Catharine Wordsworth.
[2]Gawen Mackereth.

[*46*]

Grasmere from Butterlip How, looking south, by William Green, 1804. The Rectory is visible immediately to the right of the clump of trees framed by the Church Stile and the church tower. Collection of Paul F. Betz.

something beyond what Grasmere school has been of late— He seems to be a *decent unlick'd Man.* Fanny was at Church with John[3] on Sunday & she said he gave them a *Jingling* sermon, she "never heard one that took so much hold of her in her life & she thought John would have cried, for his eyes filled with tears— it was all about wickedness"— Peggy Ash.[4] said about *faith*— but it was a *plain* & a *fine* discourse— & added that he was a very *godly* Man. He asked me this morning about some verses that he had seen upon Gough I shewed him yours— which he read, but those were not what he had seen— he then

[3] Johnny Wordsworth.
[4] Ashburner.

turned to the contents of the Vol. & found out another poem which hit his fancy & to which he turned & was proceeding to read— I thought there would be no end to this, particularly as I wanted to be with thee, & had no work in my hand, so I told him that he was welcome to put the book in his pocket— he seemed delighted & went smiling off like a shot with the book open, & ere he crossed the threshold to which I followed him he had begun to read— I was a good deal pleased with his uncouth eagerness— but he has a vulgar presbyterian look with him. It will be provoking if he does not get the school for he says he has given up much better offers for the sake of it, & he thought there had been no doubt but that it belonged to the Curacy— but he said he could do without it, & as he came with an intention to do what good he could, he will be the last person to breed contention in the parish. I shall be sorry not to make a trial of him, for certain it is, that we must immediately remove John if we do not. But this is a digression—

I look upon thy letter & I marvel how thou hast managed to write it so legibly, for there is not a word in it, that I could have a doubt about. but how is it that I have not received it sooner— It was written on *Sunday* before last— last Sunday *Morning* I rec^d. one of Dear Dorothy's written on the *Monday* & another in the evening of the same day, written on the *Thursday*; both *since* that day when my good angel put it into thy thoughts to make me so happy— Dorothy[5] has asked me more than once when she has found me this morning with thy letter in my hand "what I was crying about"— I told her that I was *so happy*— but she could not comprehend this. Indeed my love it has made me supremely blessed— it has given me a new feeling, for it is the first letter of love that has been exclusively my own— Wonder not then that I have been so affected by it. Dearest William! I am sorry about thy eye— that it is not well before now, & I am SORRY for what causes in me such pious & exulting gladness— that you cannot fully enjoy your absence from me— indeed William I feel, I *have felt* that you cannot, but it overpowers me to be told it by your own pen *I* was much

[5]Dora Wordsworth.

[*48*]

moved by the lines written with your hand in one of D's letters where you spoke of coming home thinking you "would be of great use" to me— indeed my love thou wouldst but I did not *want thee* so much *then,* as I do now that our uncomfortableness is passed away— if you had been here, no *doubt* there would have existed in me that underconsciousness that I had my *all in all* about me— *that* feeling which I have never wanted since[6] the solitary night did not separate us, except in absence; but I had not then that leisure which I ought to have & which is necessary to be actively alive to so rich a possession & to the full enjoyment of it— I *do* William & I shall to the end of my life consider this sacrifice as a dear offering of thy love, I feel it to be such, & I am grateful to thee for it but I trust that it will be the last of the kind that we shall need to make— I think it is unfeeling in the Beaumont's to propose a repetition of your visit next year; *I* had been thinking that after this, & D's long absence (if *my fortune* came in, or we were enabled from any other quarter) *we* might next venture to talk of a journey together, either into Wales or a tour into Scotland; yet at other times I feel that, those *Tendrils* that link us closer & more close to each other— the thought of both of us being absent from these dear Children (altho' they were left with a second Mother) would prevent my being completely free to enjoy myself even were I travelling alone with thee— The Baby wakes & I must leave off— —

Wed. Evening If this last sentence which I have looked back upon is not exactly in sympathy with your own heart, bear in mind that I was taken off before I had finished it— since which time I have *attempted* to go over the vale with the baby in my arms in search of a Man & horse to tend a part of the hay which is now ready— I found the sun so hot for the afternoon has been very fine, that I was obliged to give up the chase & trust to providence— if tomorrow be fair after a fair night, & we able to procure a Man & Horse we may finish tomorrow— —

[6]"I slept with" follows, but was deleted.

& we have finished! — it is now Thursday Night 9 oClock & they are I believe carrying the last Cart— last Evening I was intending to write more, but I was taken off by the Child, &, with him in my Arms, I was obliged to go in search of assistance to the hay— I succeeded— I need not here tell how or where— for I want to talk of more interesting things, but after that time till now I have not been able to say one word *to* thee. Yet my thoughts have ever been with thee— & my tongue has uttered, my lips have impressed upon & I have breathed thy name unto thy children a thousand times— to those who could in some measure understand me, & to those who have yet no knowledge what a Blessing they have in their Father, & how blessed, yea blessed above human blessedness is their Mother.—

Sarah[7] is now preparing Supper for the hay makers & as all the children were sleeping soundly I pulled out my Stockings to mend, which heaven knows stand in much need, thinking that as I should so soon be disturbed I would not attempt to write any to night, as I can not forward my letter till tomorrow, besides, it is better that I should not close this till after I know whether there be any thing for me at the post to morrow Evening which may throw light upon thy movements— but I could not sit in this room with nothing to disturb me but the sleeping baby without saying a few words to my best beloved, besides to morrow I must likewise prepare a letter for dearest Dorothy & we shall again be busy, within doors. — I must tell thee before I speak of any thing else that I am perfectly well— have no sore mouth no any thing that is bad & that I have a good appetite am always ready for my meals before they are ready for me— all these good things in spite of a great deal of fatigue— for I have never gone to bed this week without being wearied-out from head to foot— do not blame me for this, it has been unavoidable— every soul in the Valley have been fully employed— we have had much washing in consequence of this nasty disease & the Hay *was* to be attended to— but as it is over & as I am better rather than worse for it you will not lament

[7]Sarah Youdell.

over the necessity but comfort yourself with the thought that all this bustle & fatigue is over— Now, that I shall have time for it would that I could get myself fattened against your return— I am rejoiced to have such good accounts of D. I *knew* that she would enjoy herself, and that she would have been most cruelly disappointed if she had stayed behind & I was also sure that her heart was set upon going forward, in spite of her wishing to persuade herself & you to the contrary all this I *knew*, which made me unwilling to hear of your going without her, though at the time of preparation for your departure, I had most depressing misgivings about being left— for I did not feel myself strong & my heart was sick to think of Catharine having to sleep with Fanny Thank God these causes of uneasiness have never since disturbed me— for I have been upon the whole well & have scarcely ever been out of hearing of the child— without ever having felt inconvenience except 2 nights & then it was more from the novelty of the situation than from any other cause. How long will D. be absent? I shall be most anxious for your first letter from Wales for then I expect to be able to form some notion when I shall see thee— but I will not talk of this— —

The children are all well, only the 3 elder ones have worms & do not (D.[8] in particular) look well— I hope they will eat no more raspberries for I have frightened them about the worms & I shall give each a dose of Calomel on Saturday if it is fine weather— Catharine I do not think has improved much this week but she has not been so well attended— I having the little one constantly, she poor thing is obliged to follow at my skirts & this makes her fretful— it is easy to know before night by her looks & by her lameness how she has been tended thro' the day— she is however perfectly well & the *arrantest* Mischief that ever lived— as soon as she enters a room she looks round to see which is the greatest mischief she can do & off she goes to accomplish it— this is no sooner done, or prevented— but away she goes to another & so on till she is weary or till I am obliged to whip her which has often been the case for she looks

[8]Dora Wordsworth.

These miniatures are thought to depict the Wordsworths' two children, Thomas and Catharine; artist unidentified, c. 1811. The portraits were preserved with the Wordsworths' love letters among the papers of Mary Wordsworth and her son William recently acquired by the Dove Cottage Trust.

at you & proceeds in her wickedness undaunted, till you are obliged either to yield to her or *force* her to obedience— I do wish she may not grow tired of making curtseys before you see her, for she does this so prettily & looks so modest withal that you would be delighted with her I think you will not find her so lame as you imagine she is— the account I sent of her lameness was quite accurate, but it *looked* far worse upon paper than in her person— but of this you will be a better judge, who have not seen the progress than I am. W^m, my little W^m grows very fast & one thing I must tell you, for you will like him the better for it, he whets his lips exactly as John used to do & as none of the rest ever did— — We have more butterflies this year than I think I ever saw, or this study is a room more fitted to attract them than any other I ever sate in; I speak of this, because the prettiest thing I can tell you of D. is, that she wishes to be a Butterfly— Yesterday one was flying about, to the great delight of Catharine who almost exhausts herself with laughing at them, & D. followed it steadily with her eyes for a long time &

said "Mother do you wish you was a Butterfly, I do"— when I asked her why? she could only answer "that then she could do whatever she had a mind— Truly I think she has a good deal of the Butterfly in her if such are its powers. —

Sarah[9] is well, but not strong yet— We all keep clear of the itch— I have a letter from Mrs Marshall to D.[10] to answer— it is about her & your going to see them— I have heard nothing of Mr Jackson— he has been[11] buying another Estate (*overcheap*) in a shabby way in Langdale, but this they say is for the Bishop [?we] know it well, for it is the one, the highest up in Great Langdale & I passed it with thee on that memorable evening when we finished that only Tour we ever took together— it is flat land, & we passed the house in the darkness of the Evening— Mr R's[12] Cottage is to be closed in by the first of October— I am sure the Parsonage will not be ready for us & I would never have us enter an *unfinished* house of another Persons again. —

Dearest Love! I must bid thee good night— thou art yet at Coleorton & wilt not yet have retired from Company for the night— I should have written on as the Babe is not stirring, but I wish to reserve the remainder of my paper till tomorrow, for I am loth so soon to bid thee good night— may heaven bless thee & protect & give thee a prosperous journey & health & then O what a blessed meeting shall we have— remember me affectionately to Mr Blair— farewell *need I say*, I go to my bed to think of thee—

Friday Eve[g]. ½ past 9 oClock I must now finish my letter which I mean to take to the Carrier's to night— together with one which I have yet to write to Dorothy & now let me say while it is in my thoughts, that, as I can but write her a short letter; when you write to her you do not give her to understand that you have rec[d]. a longer one— this would make her uneasy— and I have not had it in my power to do any better— I

---

[9]Sarah Youdell.
[10]Dorothy Wordsworth.
[11]Mary wrote "being."
[12]The Reverend Edward Rowlandson.

have but this moment put the baby to bed— true it is, he has been there almost all day— but I have had to Iron & to pick & preserve Gooseberries &c— Give my Dearest Love to Sara[13] & tell her that I am anxious to hear from her, on the subject of my last— perhaps Jane[14] who had occasion to go to Ambleside & was to wait for the post may bring me one to night— I cannot help likewise thinking it possible there may be one from thee— at least there may be one from D. in which I certainly shall[15] a greeting from my best Love.

We all continue quite well Catharine has had a happy day— & thy own Child Tom has not been in the whining mood— He is grown more ravenous after string than ever, he now *sneaks* up-stairs into our drawers & be it tape stays laces or any thing in the likeness of string he has no mercy upon it— & then he is the exact image of Pambo when he is caught— he makes no progress at School & hates to go— I must tell you that this has been a day of heavy showers & that unless our hay had been housed yesterday probably it might have been spoiled— I am free to acknowledge that we are obliged to Mary Dawson for this, for while I was parleying with Robinson the Carrier about sparing us a Man yesterday (without which we could not have done) and he said he positively could not as they had so much hay ready themselves— she came forward & proposed to work in his field instead of a Man if he would send me one (she said she had meant to come to us) to this he agreed very kindly & the Man worked (with Mary, of *the lovers* who came forth before they were done) till after Nine oClock—. I could not help telling you this that you may rejoice with us in our good fortune— I think we have again finished before any of our Neighbours— —

Mrs Wilson is coming to see me next week & the Lloyds— this chicken-pox has been a fine lasting thing— the itch would not have done so well for us with the Brathay family for spite of it, they were coming last Sunday afternoon till they were told the Baby was in the chicken-pox. Mr W. has lost his race again, tho' Mrs W. says the Endeavour was within a few yards

---

[13]Sara Hutchinson.
[14]Jane Green.
[15]word omitted.

of the Victory at last, & was often before him— but they say Mr B. understands these matters better than Mr W. — Mr W. has often been at Astleys,[16] but he has never once called either to see me or his Godson—
Jane has just brought the letters one from S.[17] & one from Quince[18]— I have read S.'s letter tell her that Jack *did* make proper application to Judy. he told me without my mentioning her name, that the first thing he did was to go to her & this I am sure is true for he described the situation in which he found her, living in a house of S.W's where he keeps corn & other things which she has charge of & she considers herself of great use, & under obligation to him— He also spoke of her depressed & broken-spirited manner as being unfit for the charge of having Betsy if she could have been brought to take it upon herself— I could not but feel this to be just for I thought the same when I last saw her in company with Tom & W. who may if you ask them give you their opinion— If Jack did not tell me a *positive lie* Nancy died while He was in London & Mrs H gave him the first intelligence by letter— You should not rely so much upon George's word— I do not want to persuade you or Myself that Miss W.[19] is a proper person or that J. has not acted most improperly but I do not wish to see Sara (for I recollect that it is not to her that I am writing) give to him more blame (alas! she needs not) than he deserves— tell her likewise that I do not think any person (Nancy being gone) whom we should think it right to place Betsy with would chuse her to cook for them— nothing else she complains of— Now for Q's letter— it is a very entertaining one dated London 30 July & he says he is going to set off that day for Wrington, where he will stay about a fortnight— *abouts!* Tell S. that I could not have undertaken the care of *all* the Children at the sea-side with only *one* Ser[vt]. & if I had taken *both* what was to become of the cows, gar[den] (& Hay if I had gone while Jane was here) we could not afford to give those away

---

[16]Mary wrote "Ashleys."
[17]Sara Hutchinson.
[18]Thomas De Quincey.
[19]Miss Weir.

Ask S. if she has any idea what can be done for Betsy if Miss W. does not answer— [?well ?I ?know ?that ?it ?would] be most foolish either to irritate Jack or Miss W. who has a great spirit & would [?temperate] Betsy

I did not think thus to conclude my letter— May God bless th[ee]

I observe that Q's letter, after having told me at the end of it that he kept his resolution of setting out on that day, 31st J. is dated by him *on* the outside Aug 1st!! farewell my blessing—

I will write to dearest Sara as soon as I have time— but I have many letters to write— Bless you & her & all of them

3

William to Mary, 11 August 1810

On 6 August William left Coleorton, accompanied by Beaumont. The two were enthusiastic landscape gardeners—William had designed the winter garden at Coleorton—and Sir George was eager to show him the Leasowes, formerly the home of the poet William Shenstone and renowned for its picturesque gardens. After parting from Beaumont, William visited Alexander Blair just outside Birmingham and called at the home of the elder Lloyds, where his brother Christopher and his family were guests. Christopher was then rector and dean of Bocking, Essex, and domestic chaplain to Charles Manners-Sutton, the archbishop of Canterbury, at Lambeth Palace, London. He had married Priscilla Lloyd in 1804; epilepsy and insanity ran in her family, and she herself suffered from nervous debilities.

Dorothy Wordsworth remained at Coleorton until 10 August, when she set out alone for Bury St. Edmunds and another round of visits.

William proceeded southward, and as he caught sight of the Malvern Hills he thought of Joseph Cottle, the Bristol bookseller, who had published Wordsworth's and Coleridge's *Lyrical Ballads* in 1798 and in the same year produced a volume of his own poetry, titled *Malvern Hills*. Racedown Lodge in north Dorset had been the home of William and Dorothy Wordsworth from September 1795 to July 1797, and Mary had been their guest from the end of November 1796 to early June 1797.

Health continues to be a subject of concern in the letters. Though not inactive, Mary's sisters Sara and Joanna Hutchinson, then at Hindwell, appear to have been frequently underweight and understrength. William's inflammation of the eyelids persisted, and he complained of bad digestion and hemorrhoids

SCOTLAND

Newcastle o

Penrith   Bishop Middleham
Keswick o   o Appleby   o Stockton
        Grasmere   o Sockburn
          o Kendal   Gallow Hill •   o Scarborough

        o Lancaster   o York

                o Manchester
          o Liverpool

          ∿o Chester
                      ENGLAND

        o Oswestry
              Ashby de le Zouch
WALES   o Shrewsbury   • Coleorton
                              o Leicester
                    o Birmingham
    Knighton o   o Ludlow
    Presteigne o o Kington   Worcester   Cambridge   o Bury St.
    Hudwell   o   o Stratford-upon-Avon   Edmunds
    New Radnor o   o MALVERN HILLS
    Hay-on-Wye o   o Hereford   o Bocking
              o Ross-on-Wye
    Abergavenny o o Monmouth   o Oxford
        Tintern o   London
        Chepstow o   o
                o Bristol   Windsor o

        • Racedown

                              0   50 MILES

England and Wales

(euphemistically referred to as his "old enemy"), both familiar disorders for him. Mary had been distressed by an infection in the mouth, and William solicitously urged her to doctor herself with the remedy prescribed by the local apothecary and physician, Richard ("Dr. Dick") Scambler of Ambleside.

Mary Monkhouse, cousin of Mary Wordsworth, was the godmother of Tommy Wordsworth. The Addisons were old family friends. Richard Addison had joined Wordsworth's elder brother Richard, a London solicitor, as a partner at law, and Isabella Addison had married John Monkhouse, brother of Mary Monkhouse, in 1806 but died the following year. John subsequently farmed with Tom Hutchinson at Hindwell and, after Tom's marriage, nearby at Stowe.

Hindwell— Saturday August 11th
I arrived here at 10 this morning; where I found all well, Sara wonderfully improved in look and Joanna quite fat, Sara indeed also. The House is comfortable, and its situation beside the pool, and the pool itself quite charming, and far beyond my expectation. Having said this, let me turn at once to thee my love of loves and to thy dearest of Letters which I found here, and read with a beating heart. O my blessing, how happy was I in learning that my Letter had moved thee so deeply, and thy delight in reading had if possible been more exquisite than mine in writing. You seem to have been surprized at the receipt of my Letter, and surely it is odd that I did not mention to you I should avail myself of some opportunity, and as strange that you did not take for granted that I should. My Letter had been written three or four days before I could find the means of sending it off, which was the reason of its arriving so late; you would notice also that it was somewhat worn, for I had carried it about with me in my pocket. — I was sure that you would be most happy in receiving from me such a gift from the whole undivided heart for your whole & sole posses-

sion; and the Letter in answer which I have received from you today I will entrust to your keeping when I return, and they shall be deposited side by side as a bequest for the survivor of us. Every day every hour every moment makes me feel more deeply how blessed we are in each other, how purely how faithfully how ardently, and how tenderly we love each other; I put this last word last because, though I am persuaded that a deep affection is not uncommon in married life, yet I am confident that a lively, gushing, thought-employing, spirit-stirring, passion of love, is very rare even among good people. I will say more upon this when we meet, grounded upon recent observation of the condition of others. We have been parted my sweet Mary too long, but we have not been parted in vain, for wherever I go I am admonished how blessed, and almost peculiar a lot mine is. —

You praised the penmanship of my last; I could wish that this should be legible also, but I fear I shall wish in vain; for I must write in a great hurry having only an hour allotted to me. Let me then first communicate the facts in which you may be interested, relating to my journey &c otherwise if I give way to the emotions of my heart first you will hear nothing of these. — On Monday morn: at 9 o'clock Sir G. B. and I left Ashby in a chaise. Sir G— had a wish to see the Leasowes with me; I had never been there and he had not seen the place these thirty years; I reserve the detail of this journey till we meet. We slept the first night at Hagley returned to Birmingham next day at 4 afternoon, went together to the play, and the next morning walked about the Town, and I accompanied Sir G. back on his way as far as four miles which brought me to within 2 miles a 1/2 of Castle Bromwich, Mr Blairs. At Mr Blairs, I found a note from my B^r Chris^r who had accidentally heard of my intention of being at Mr Blairs. I was greatly surprized at this, as I had confidently concluded that he was either gone from Birm: or had never come thither from his not having answered the Letter inviting him to Coleorton. On Thursday he came over to Mr Blairs, dined with us, and I returned with him, and supped at Lloyds, where I found Priscilla looking I thought not very well. The children were gone to bed and asleep so of course I can have no accurate image of them: their faces were heated and they seemed bloomed, but their natural complexions, are sallow. The eldest is the handsomest, much, the 2nd the stoutest, and the third the plainest; so it appeared as they slept and so, I was told, it is; Christopher looked uncommonly; but I am sorry to say that he is likely to have great trouble, at least I fear so) from the state of his wifes health and the nature of her malady; great expense also which at present he can ill bear,— for his living has entangled him in two law suits; and you will grieve to hear that he has been much deceived as the income of it; it is some hundreds lower than he had reason to expect, so that he will be not a little pinched, unless it should please God to take the Bishop. But not a word of these particulars to any body.

On friday Morning, I was called a little after three, having had two hours feverish sleep, got on the top of the Coach, it began to rain before we were out of Birming: and rained for two hours and a half; my umbrella & coat however protected me pretty well; when we were half way to Worcester the weather cleared up and I had a pleasant ride through a fine Country to that City, which stands charmingly upon the Severn, at no great distance from the Malvern hills. These hills which are a fine object brought Joseph Cottle to my mind, and dearest Dorothy, who had travelled this way when she came from Newcastle to meet me at Bristol whence we journeyd to Racedown; but though much endeared to me on this latter account, I looked at them with a trembling which I cannot describe when I thought that *you* had not seen them, but *might* have seen, if you had but taken the road through Bristol when you left Racedown; in which case I should certainly have accompanied you as far as Bristol; or further, perhaps: and then I thought, that you would not have taken the coach at Bristol, but that you would have walked on Northwards with me at your side, till unable to part from each other we might have come in sight of those hills which skirt the road for so many miles, and thus continuing our journey (for we should have moved on at small expense) I fancied that we should have seen so deeply into each others hearts, and been so fondly locked in each others arms, that we should have braved the worst and parted no more. Under that tree, I thought as I passed along we might have rested, of that stream might have drank, in that thicket we might have hidden ourselves from the sun, and from the eyes of the passenger; and thus did I feed on the thought of bliss that might have been, which would have [been] intolerable from the force of regret had I not felt the happiness which waits me when I see you again. O Mary I love you with a passion of love which grows till I tremble to think of its strength; your children and the care which they require must fortunately steal between you and the solitude and the longings of absence— when I am moving about in travelling I am less unhappy than when stationary, but then I am at every moment, I will not say reminded of you, for you never I think are out of my mind 3 minutes together however I am engaged, but I am every moment seized with a longing wish that you might see the objects which interest me as I pass along, and not having you at my side my pleasure is so imperfect that after a short look I had rather not see the objects at all. But I must return to my journey. I left Worcester at half past ten, reached Leominster at 5, and there was 20 miles to Hindwell, without coach— Luckily two other persons were going part of the same way; so we took chaise for 14 miles, I slept at Presteigne 5 miles from hence, hired a guide who bore my luggage, and I arrived here before eleven.

I have read to Sara the parts of your Letter intended for her, and all the rest which I could read; she will reply to these of course herself. How happy am I [to] learn that thou art so well, and untormented with that cruel pain in thy mouth! May it never return! if it does fail not to apply to Dr Dicks remedies: for my account for really I have suffered much in this cruel complaint of thine— I have thought of it ten thousand times since we parted & sometimes I have fancied that I was caressing thee, and thou couldst not meet me with kindred delight and rapture from the interruption[1] of this distressing pain. But far oftener for less selfish reasons has it employed my 'mind

---

[1] William wrote "interrupted."

with an anxiety which I cannot describe; for every thing about you that is indicative of weakness or derangement of health affects me when I [am] absent from you, and cannot see how you look, beyond what it is in the power of words to describe. O take care of yourself for all our sakes— but I cannot bear to look that way, and I know you will do nothing to hurt yourself for my sake. —

My stomach failed about a fortnight since from too much talking, or rather from not being sufficiently alone— before I left C—[2] by taking more care I brought it about; and except in my eyelids I look well, and am well; but certainly though not weak far from being so strong as I should have been but for my old enemy: that has troubled me more than ever. — I agree with you that it was unreasonable in the B's[3] to expect me to go to C— again next summer; be assured, I shall not do it on any account nor will I go any where without thee. I cannot but think knowing how the little ones would be taken care of but that we might be happy supremely happy together in a tour of a few weeks if our circumstances would allow; but this will never, I fear be the case, nor am I anxious about this; but I never will part from you for more than a week or a *fort*night at the very utmost, unless when I [am] compelled by a sense of duty that leaves no choice— I can not and ought not; if I could lay in a stock of health and strength to enable me to work more vigorously when I return there might be some plea for this but the contrary is the case; for my longing day and night to see you again is more powerful far, as I said before than[4] when you were at Middleham; and when I am away from you I seem to have heart for nothing and no body else— But this theme is endless; I must content myself with your Letters for a short time; and oh most dearly shall I prize them, till I consign them to your care to be preserved whatever else we lose.

I have not yet said a word about the time I purpose to stay here; but I came with a resolution not to extend it beyond a fortnight, for a hundred reasons which will crowd in upon

[2]Coleorton.
[3]Beaumonts.
[4]William wrote "that."

your mind. At all events I shall move heaven and earth to be with you by this day three weeks. I shall not stop a moment at Liverpool more than I can help, if I go that way. You may guess how eager I am to be at home, when I tell you that Christophers entreaties and my own wishes, could not prevail upon me to stay half a day at Birmingham. — Certainly I parted from him with great regret, as he and I are likely to be so much divided. I will satisfy Sara's claim upon me and let me add a little too for Joanna and Mary Monkhouse especially, and then I shall take wing and oh for the sight of dear Grasmere, and how I shall pant up the hill, and then for dear little W. and his beloved Mother, and how shall we pour out hearts together in the lonely house, and in the lonely and to *us* thrice dear Season.

Thank you for your pretty tales of Dorothy and strin[g]-loving Thomas; bless [him] he shall be contented if possible, I will bring him string from his Godmother, string for his Uncle, for Mr Addison and for myself adieu adieu adieu, for I am told I have not a moment to lose, and that the post will be lost— this must not be again & again farewell— a thousand kisses for you all, yourself first, John Dorothy, Thomas, Catharine, W^m. dear little Catharine I have not mentioned her, but she has often been here in my thoughts again & again farewell— I fear for her Take care

4

Mary to William, 14 August 1810

Mary continued to ponder how her sister Betsy might best be looked after. The solution she suggested here would have put Betsy in the care of Tamar Turner, sister of the Wordsworths' servant Fanny Turner; Tamar soon moved to Yewdale, however, and Betsy was settled under the tactful supervision of a Mrs. Elstob. The woeful change in Grasmere that Mary and Tamar bewailed was caused by the rowdy Astley clan.

Several of Mary's remarks disclose that the Wordsworths had begun their search for another house. One option was the Grasmere parsonage, or rectory, which stood unoccupied in disrepair. From 1808, when they moved to Allan Bank, the house had proved inhospitable to the Wordsworths. They camped out in the large rooms, which they had neither sufficient furniture nor carpets to make comfortable. The house was cold and the chimneys smoked. Dorothy recalled one particularly grim event in their first winter:

> There was one stormy day in which we could have no fire but in my Brother's Study—and that chimney smoked so much that we were obliged to go to bed with the Baby [Catharine] in the middle of the day to keep it warm, and I, with a candle in my hand, stumbled over a chair, unable to see it. [*MY*, I, 280]

Eyes smarted, and "dishes [were] washed, and no sooner set into the pantry than they [were] covered with smoke" (*MY*, I, 281). Workmen came and went for a year; the chimneys were raised three feet—all to no avail.

Mr. and Mrs. Ford North of Liverpool occupied Rydal Mount,

the home to which the Wordsworths moved in 1813, when they left Grasmere vale. Mrs. North had earned a reputation for being snobbish and meddlesome.

Mary's callers were Charles Lloyd, Jr., of Brathay, son of the Birmingham banker, and Lieutenant Thomas Southey, younger brother of the poet Robert Southey. With his family Robert Southey occupied one half of Greta Hall, Keswick, and the Coleridges the other, though Coleridge himself was rarely present. (In 1808 Coleridge had separated from his wife.) Edith Fricker Southey and Sara Fricker Coleridge were sisters. Derwent Coleridge, nearly ten, was the third of the Coleridges' sons. The Southeys' new baby was Katharine.

Mrs. M., whose visit Mary anticipated, was Anna Benson Skepper Montagu, third wife of William's friend Basil Montagu. The Wordsworths disliked her, and on William's advice Dorothy did not return to Grasmere until after the Montagus' departure in mid-October.

George and Sarah Green died in a storm on 19 March 1808 on their way home from a sale in the neighboring valley of Langdale. Eight children were left orphans, and the Wordsworths helped to raise and administer funds for their support. Dorothy and De Quincey both wrote moving accounts of the incident.

Tuesday Aug 14th.

My dearest Love.

I begin upon this Letter because I think I can by means of a new pen make it contain as much as I shall be able to write before Jane[1] sets off to Kendal on her way to Appleby, by whom I shall forward this— Upon Jack's letter I can only say that I am very sorry that Betsy's mind should have been disturbed— because we ought all to have borne in mind the consequence of this— I have avoided writing to her much against

[1]Jane Green.

my own feelings, merely on this account— I pray that the matter *may* rest till Dorothy goes which I would have her to do by all means— Sara first writing to her stating all her objections to Miss W. & her ideas of what can be done for Betsy provided she is removed— D. knows my feelings— & nothing new has struck me since you went away, except that last night while Mary J. & I were sitting at Tamar's where we drank Tea— I thought when T. was regetting leaving her house, (as most likely she will have to do) that if we should buy it, we might fix B. in it with T. for a *Governante*— but I fear that T. is too *narvee* to manage poor Betsy, for we all know there is much truth in what Jack says about her. — I had a letter from Dorothy yesterday afternoon telling me that thou my beloved wert gone— & from her two last letters, which I was much surprized to receive from Ashby, I was grieved to find that you were disappointed in not having more letters from me before you left Coleorton— this was entirely owing to a mistake D. led me into in her letter written upon the 26th. of July which she concluded by saying "certainly I shall be at Bury or on my road thither this day se'night"— viz. the 2^d. of Aug.— now, calculating upon these her *last words* rather than upon what she had before stated in her letter, I concluded that no letter written after the day upon which I received this, they having always been so long upon the road, could reach Coleorton before you left it on the 6th. of Aug. much less in time for D., therefore I forwarded letters to your several places of destination— D. would meet with 2 at Bury— but as I had hoped for a letter— another heart feeding letter— from thee as soon as thou hadst begun to move I deferred writing a *second* letter till that blessed one might reach me— I have hitherto received none; but I must no longer delay giving thee information concerning home— & happy am I to be able to send good news— for we are at present *all* well—

Sarah[2]— after another week's illness, is now I hope in a way to get finally well— the change we looked for having taken place. — I am perfectly well & stand in no need of Dr Dick's prescriptions which dear D. has sent to me & the children are

[2]Sarah Youdell.

all well— I have tied Catharine's left Arm down to make her use her right, which she is perfectly capable to do, more free- ly— this does not make her the least unhappy & I think the confinement causes her to walk more straight— she gets more tumbles it is true— but I think it is better that it should be done now, while, having been accustomed only to use *one* hand, it is less of a distress to her to part with the other than it will be hereafter, & certainly there is a better chance *now* to cure her of her left-handedness— Whining Tom begins to look better, & the Baby is a Darling— He is the quietest Creature ever borne, & he will talk presently. Cath. is terribly jealous of him— she would not care what became of him provided she could put him off my knee— John is quite happy again in the prospect of going on with Gowan who is still Schoolmaster— Madam North has persuaded him not to give up the school to spite Parson Jackson no doubt who I suppose cannot turn him out without the interference of the Parish which they are by no means inclined to do— I do not think we shall be tempted to take the Parsonage unless all is done that we require if we have no school— & I have been looking in my own mind to the house [b]eside Appleby or to the Parsonage at Hawkshead. — there are a thousand objections to the Parsonage which will make us regret it the less & I am sure if these reptiles harbour here we shall lament the change in Grasmere so much that it will be well to be removed from the sight of it. As Tamar says "this horn's *crowning* at all hours & you are in danger of being over run upon the roads". —

I have been interrupted by Lloyd & T. Southey— Ll. told me that thou supped with his Father & wert well last Thursday Ev^{ng}— my heart beat with gladness to *hear* of thee from any one; though thou always pretends to be well to strangers so I do not reckon much upon that part of it— neither was I happy to find thee at Bir:[3] on *Thursday*— D. had told me that thou wert to be at Hindwell on the Wed: so I had calculated that *one week* of thy stay thither was over— Dearest love! I am happy to

[3] Birmingham.

[*68*]

Grasmere, looking northwest, by Joseph Farington, c. 1810. Immediately left of the church the Church Stile is visible; the Rectory is on its left. Allan Bank rises on the hill behind them. Pavement End is at the far left. Collection of Beth Darlington.

think thou art with dear Sara, yet I tremble at every joint to think of our meeting & of the *possibilities* that may prevent it— I am sick at the thought— O what would not I give to see thee for one moment! — Lloyd has pleased me by telling me, what I rather wish I had heard from some one more to be depended upon, that he never "saw me look so well in his life"— I should not wonder if this is true, for he spoke it as if it was a thing that flashed upon him when we were talking nothing about it & T. S. echoed his words— To be sure I had popped on my laced cap before I went down to them which might make a change in my appearance or I have myself fancied I was become like nobody in my looks and appearance— I believe the fine folks at the church style fancy as I pass with the Baby in my Arms that I am a shabby Nurse Maid at the great house— for they brush or gallop past me without ever such a thought seeming to enter their head as, that I am a Gentleman's wife— Certainly my *dress* does not entitle me to much respect— I must have a new Bonnet to appear in before Mrs M. comes, so as D. will not be at home in time thou must bring me one— Sara may give you directions about it— I have had none since she went so she can tell what will suit me— At Liverpool you must order for us a Cask of rice & another of oil. do not neglect this & enquire of Mr Crump about that money which he collected for the Green's— & if you *can*, bring it, you may tell him that having to pay for one of them as an apprentice & the rest of their money, being in the stocks it will be very convenient to have his— now pray do this— I have had a deal of trouble about their affairs— the Parish want their Legacies from them & have refused to go on with their payment to the persons with whom the children are lodged. —

We now seem to be so comfortable. Sarah[4] having got better & able to work, & I do think that Fanny is capable of being the best Servant in the world, she has gone thro' the whole work of the house during S.'s illness with so much spirit & activity as has quite delighted me & has kept the Kitchens *like Paradise*— Yet— they are both going to leave us— & for what?— not because they want more wages, for I told them that should each have a guinea a year more in consideration that Jane was going & that they would have the Shoes &. to clean— not because they were not happy, in their places— for they both say that they never were *so happy*, nor do they expect to be more so— but, Fanny goes, because we are not to keep 3 servants, &, because she wants to see different ways"— & Sarah goes because "Fanny is going, & as they came together, they will go together". I have said quite as much to them to shew them their folly as became me, so I shall not ask them further to stay. I think far worse of S. than I do of F. because I am certain from positive reasons that *she* never thought of leaving us till this whim of Fannys put it into her head— & that she should determine to leave her place at this time after having been

[4]Sarah Youdell.

treat[ed] with as much tenderness during her illness as if she had been my own child shews a coldness of heart that hurts me to think about. — I am sorry we are going to lose them for I know that we shall find it difficult to meet with others to suit us as well as they do. —

Mrs Southey has got a daughter— & poor Derwent has broken his arm, but it is doing well— these things happened above a fortnight ago but I only heard them from Ll. for a letter & parcel of Mrs C's[5] has been lost— T. S. says that D. scarcely suffered any thing— it was snappd somewhere between the elbow & wrist by falling of a plank— Ll. also repeated some lies that C.[6] had told him, but which I did not notice sufficiently to report particularly, about a metaphisical work that he *had sent* to the press & about a *long letter* which he had written to him— neither of which had ever been done to any person's knowledge— he must be, as Ll. says, insane— —

We have had most beautiful weather— Yet terrible for the hay— nobody having got much in except ourselves, greatest part of it must be spoiled we have had such heavy rains— but never continued— never has a day passed upon which you might not have, at some part of it, enjoyed the Country— — Yesterday I think was the first day that I have left the house except upon business, or to air one of the children since you went away & when I sauntered alone behind Tamars Cottage after Tea my soul was filled with the beauty that was around me blended with the thoughts of you & the dreams of the delight which might be ours & our childrens were that ground but ours— & you may be sure I was most happy Dearest William! — while I was writing these last words my little darling Catharine rouzed me by crying, & calling at the stairs foot Mam, Mam, Mamma, I have fetched her up & put her upon the bed with a stock of "Prettys" but she will not be happy without tossing her things down & then being after them & up again so I must try to be *rid of her* before I finish— I have left Catharine but so unhappy that I must hasten to the end of my

[5]Sara Coleridge.
[6]Coleridge.

letter. — I do not recollect that I have any thing more to say than to beg you to write soon and at length that I may know what you are doing— & desire Sara to tell me how your eye looks & if *she* thinks you are well— D. told me *you* had been better but that your eye was still weak when you left her— I know not whether you are much further from me than when you were at Coleorton, but I *feel* as if you were, far *nearer* to me, & this feeling encreases my anxiety for your being still nearer— & so on will it now be till I have you in my arms & this void filled up which I always feel, (without knowing exactly what ails me) in your absence— —

The Children are delighted to hear that you are soon to be at home— John particularly, who puts on his sweet & says "but *how* soon Mother"— What a pity but that this sweet Lad should be in the way to be a good Scholar— The new Curate is one of Whitelocks deciples— he has been off to visit him, perhaps to get a fresh stock of Sermons— I rather think he will make an impression in the parish God love you my best beloved. thy own faithful & affectionate Wife

M Wordsworth

5

Mary to William, 15–19 August 1810

Mary's crowded program allowed her no holiday on 16 August, her fortieth birthday, shared with Dora's sixth, but she seems to have been serenely cheerful while exemplifying the worn maxim that woman's work is never done. A passing note of wistfulness sounds only when she recalls that William once likened her "dusky hair" to Twilight's and that time has faded it to grey.

Butterlip How, which Mary eyed so hopefully, is a wooded hill near the center of Grasmere—a fine piece of property. Thomas and Elizabeth King lived at the Hollins, Grasmere. Mr. Wilcock was a local auctioneer and estate agent. The Reverend Thomas Jackson, rector of Grasmere parish, also served as agent for the Rydal Hall estates, owned by the Fleming family. Mr. Simpson was probably John Simpson of Nab Cottage, on Rydal Water. De Quincey confessed to being "blindingly, doatingly, in a servile degree, devoted" to Catharine Wordsworth (Masson, II, 442–443), and while his purse was far too light for him to purchase Butterlip How, he told Mary that he wished he might buy it as a "birthday present" for Dora and Catharine (Jordan, p. 259). Mr. S. was Richard Scambler, "Dr. Dick," the apothecary at Ambleside.

Mary played hostess to John Wilson of Elleray, on Windermere, his mother, two sisters (Jane, the elder, and Elizabeth), and Jane Penny. Miss Penny, the daughter of a wealthy Liverpool merchant, was acclaimed the belle of the Lakes, and despite Mary's tart estimate of her mother wit, she married Wilson the following May. The guests lodged at opposite sides of Grasmere vale, Miss Wilson and Miss Penny at Dove Cottage, with Mr. Wilson just across the road at the Ashburners', and the remainder of the party at Allan Bank. Ganny was the Wordsworth children's name for Peggy Ashburner.

Hartley Coleridge was the eldest son of Samuel Taylor Coleridge. A warm, good-humored boy of fourteen, he was adored by the Wordsworth children.

Wed. morn Aug 15th

My dearest William
   I sent off a letter by Jane Green yesterday & have yet received none from you since you left Coleorton, but I cannot help writing to talk about Butterlip how— I am sadly fearful we shall let it slip, I would, poor as we are rather give a *few hundreds* too much than that it should fall into bad hands— If — — and if— you may depend upon it £200 beyond what you bid will not prevent my striking a bargain without you— Mrs King was here last night— she is most anxious as is her husband to keep out those creatures who are likely to spoil the place. they have written to Mr Crump, thinking he might perhaps purchase it— Mr Wilcock is authorized to sell it privately before the day of sale. if he can come at the price Mr J. has put upon it— M^r. K. bid him I know not whether seriously or not, twelve hundred pounds— but Mr W. said he had 13 or 14 hundred already bidden & I think he said that *fifteen* would not buy it— But twelve hundred is what Mr K. thinks it is fairly worth without considering the situation— The day of Sale is not yet fixed but M^r. K. is sure it might be bought for much less before that time. Mr Simpson thinks that Jackson will never see his own money again unless he waits till it strikes the fancy of some one, not if he makes an *actual* sale— You must positively be here at the Sale— Mr Crump no doubt will, so he may come with you, but I am sure he will not bid till you are done. I must inform Mr de Q. that we may know how far *he* will go— but I should hate him to have it (unless indeed he would entail it upon our Catharine) he could be so invited & make such calculations— his trees he would reckon upon as he does upon his books— & value them upon the same principle.

Thomas De Quincey, by Sir John Watson-Gordon, c. 1845. The Dove Cottage Trust, Grasmere.

Perhaps Fanny & Catharine may find a letter from you at Ambleside— yesterday was so wet we had no communication *from* the Post— this is a sweet morning after a most heavenly moon light night & Fanny is going to take Cath: to have a sore finger dressed by Mr S.— we may thank God if we get out of this house with the children alive— for those flapping doors are so dangerous— on Monday she was sitting upon the back

door steps & the door flappd to when she had her hand some
way or other behind her (as I understand from Sis:[1]) Jane told
me at the time simply that she had fallen & cut her finger—
she did not cry much & it was covered with blood, so I thought
the best thing I could do was to tie it up with the tincture & let
it remain a few days— but last night she rested so ill in consequence of the uneasiness it gave her, that I opened it out this
Morning & found it a very ugly cut & bruise— the finger
almost laid open & proud flesh in to[o], so I think proper to have
it dressed by Mr S. & get proper direction about it— it is well it
is the left hand, & glad am I that her hand was not tied down
when it happened (tho' if it had been tied, it could not have
happened) or I should have thought had she not been confined this would not have been— I shall not again confine her
arm, for fear of her hurting herself by a fall, but, when the
finger is well, muffle the Hand & leave the arm at liberty— at
present the weak hand is the more useful one. —

Thursday— no letter yesterday— all the time of my little
Darlings absence I pleased myself with the image of her coming to me, (from this her first visit to Ambleside) in bustling
haste as if poor Lamb she would be down at every step, but
with such gladness on her countenance, & a letter from her
Father in her hand— but no, she returned through heavy rain
without one— but so overjoyed that she put the whole house
into such spirits! — It is truly wonderful to see what an effect
being much in the air has upon this child, she is always a merry
creature, but when she is much out of doors she seems to be
almost crazy with happiness— What a pity then is it that this
abominable itch, Sarah's illness & other causes, should neces-
sarily have prevented her going out, except for a short time
together & without the advantage of shewing her fresh objects— for it is so plain to be seen the good effect that this has
upon her mind, it could not but be the best thing to strength-
en her body & tend to restore her limbs to their full power
far beyond any other means— You cannot think what a rest-

[1]Dora Wordsworth.

less mortal I was while she was absent— the house seemed to have lost all its life— One thing I must tell you that fanny was stopped upon the road by 2 Gentlemen who asked whose beautiful little Girl she was. Her sore finger will be a trifle— though it [is] a very very deep cut— but it looked so bad in consequence of having been badly tied up— the blood & fear of giving her pain, prevented my seeing which was the right way to close the wound— —

Thursday afternoon Mary J. & I have been since I wrote the above to walk with the 4 younger Children & upon our return Sarah put your 2^d. dear letter into my hand— Dinner was waiting— Fanny gone to Coniston to the funeral of a little child of her B^r the Baby not asleep Cath: wanting attendance— & your letter! I made dinner wait till I had read to where you begin with the account of your Journey— passed over all that, & the recital of thy feelings, (which afterwards made me tremble too) at the thought of our journey thro' Worstershire which *might have been*)— till I came to the concluding paragraph which I read— then dispatchd our Lamb, peas & potatoes & after helping Mary & the children to their pudding I took the baby from Sarah & (while they finished their meal) with him at the breast I read from first to last of this letter which tells me so many blessed truths— & which further tells me the time of thy return— The 1st of September is the day thou mentions but perhaps you may not exactly come upon the day— but about that time— with what anxious delight shall I expect my Love! — they will not let me go on— Cath: is cross today; she is about her two *last* teeth— when those are out, which I trust will [be] the case before thy return I shall dismiss her from my bed without fear— I *must* go to her— —

Struck 12 oClock. I have been sitting up till this hour to finish a pair of Trousers for John, but I can not go to bed (I am come into my own room & the Baby will be here in a moment) without wishing thee good night— I have now lived over my fortieth birth day, (*our* birth day, as little Dorothy says one day she said to me "Don't you wish Mother, it was father's birth day too." —) & I am at this moment as well, and to my own feelings have as much Life, spirit & activity about me as when I was 20 years of age— tis true I am losing my teeth & my hair is becoming grey— these, the two great ornaments my Youth had to boast of, (my hair especially I prized, because thou once ventured to speak in admiration of it) I must own are *upon the wain* — else I think I am as good as ever— & every body now begins to tell me how well I look— & I believe in my own heart that this improvement began in me on the day that I received thy letter, & this leads me to speak of the one that this day has brought— My little Catharine, if I durst have ventured her 3 hours later at Ambleside yesterday might have been the little Mercury that brought me this treasure— but I must not go on now but prepare to receive my little William— Perhaps I shall finish my letter in the Morning— in the afternoon the Wilsons are coming—

Sat: Morning 12 oClock I was obliged to hurry into bed on thursday Night. & much as I wished to have forwarded this letter by the Carrier this morning I had not a moments leisure throughout the day yesterday to finish it— for Fannys being from home the day before till late in the Evening caused both her time & Saras' to be taken up all this day in giving a thorough cleaning to the study, the window is cleaned for I know Mr Wilson would prefer it to all the other rooms for our visitors to sit in— At four oClock, before I was quite ready to receive them came Mrs the 2 Miss W^s Miss Jane Penny & Mr W.— in consequence of Quince having offered them his Cot-[tage]— the beds were prepared there for Miss W. & Miss Jane— & Mr W. to be in attendance, ordered his bed at Peggy Ash:^{s}— After drinking Tea in the study they went out to walk leaving me to put my young ones to bed— after which we all repaired to the Cottage where we had a neat little supper, some of Quince's wine & a snug fire in the Parlour— this all went off very pleasantly,— we staid as long as *I* durst, then Mrs W. Miss E. Mary J & I came here & just as I set my foot upon the threshold my little Darling began to cry. I took him from the place where I had left him, he had not stirred during my ab-

Dove Cottage, Town End, Grasmere, by Amos Green, c. 1805. The Ashburners' cottage and the carrier's stable are on the left. The Dove Cottage Trust, Grasmere.

sence— but he *is* the sweetest quietest creature ever born— they all came up to Breakfast (& I gave them a very nice one) & have departed very well pleased with their visit, I dare say, as you will hear when you call at Elleray on your return— you must call— for your own sake, (& Mrs W. desired I would tell you so) great as your haste [w]ill be & tremblingly anxious as I shall be, guessing you to be so near— Mr W. would like much to join you [   ] day, or days at Ambleside interfere— I doubt indeed Mr W. will marry Miss Jane. & O she is [   ] Person & her countenance belies her if her mind is not made of lard— Mr W. would like this to be— I am sure it would undo him, but more of this when we meet.

Your beloved letter my William I never can be enough grateful to thee for— O William! I really am too happy to move about on this earth, it *is well* indeed that my employments keep me active about other things or I should not be able to contain my felicity— Good Heavens! that I should be adored in this manner by thee thou first & best of Men, is a lot so far beyond, not only all my hopes but all my desires & the blessing is so weighty it is so *solemnly great* that it would be even *painful* were I left to brood much upon the thought of it. I therefore feel a comfort in those salutary interruptions that will only admit of that delightful, happy chearing thought of thee which I can communicate to the children & which they can in part enter into. — Our Conversations now are all of your return— John is certainly most anxious to see you for your *own sake*— Tom for what you can do for him, & Sis. in part, I own, for her love of you but she looks to the ribbon you have for her (tho' she thinks it is rather a useless thing)— The Ladies were enraptured with her beauty, but she behaved as she always does, after the first shyness was past, when her Lover is here Miss W. is faithful to John. but Tot.[2] stole all their hearts by his quietness— they little know what a whiner he is— Mrs W. was astonished to see Cath: so well, tho' I have not quite been in such good heart about her lately, on this account, that now when the air is become cool, the arm (which is not covered with Flannel as the leg is) is colder than the other & turns blue— I find that we must keep it constantly covered; pray desire Sara to send by you some Stockings of Welsh wool for all the children if she can not procure any let her send yarn— but if she could send Stockings only for C. it would be well as I wish to put them on immediately & I shall have no time to knit till after dear D's return— Mrs W. said W.[3] was exactly like John when she first saw him, only J. had no cap on— I do not think W. at all like what John was now— he is not so handsome as he was, when you went away—

C. would not suffer me to write on in the morning— she is *terribly* fond of me, & Fanny being busy does not try to keep her from following & crying after me, I therefore left off writing much against my inclination & with the Baby & Mary J.

[2] Tommy Wordsworth.
[3] Willy Wordsworth.

(who is so happy here that she never talks of going home) I went down to see if I could send to the Post, to know if there was a letter from Dorothy, (I did not expect one from thee) as Hartley had called to enquire but the *barber* who is the letter Man at Ambleside was gone to shave Mr Peddar & the letters could not be come at— We reached Mary Dawsons at 2 oClock, not having dined, when it began to rain & has rained heavily ever since— I waited till 6 oClock watching its clearing up in vain, so with Ganny's blue Cloak & the Baby under it I came home for I could not rest without seeing all put to bed— Mary is left behind & Hartley is gone to carry her my Clogs to walk in— I had a delightful walk thro' the rain the torrants were roaring & the Mountains streaming with the heaviness of the rain, but the cloak protected the baby & o how I wished thou couldst but have met me & seen the oddness of my appearance— my White Stockings & petticoat looked so ridiculous from under the short blue Cloak that only just covered the Baby in my arms. I have been much affected by Hartley's attention to us— he refused Mrs Wilson's invitation to Elleray today because he had not first been here— this is a proof of H's feelings beyond what I have before seen— he looks very well & is in good spirits— Derwent mends. —

This day fortnight[4] at this hour (I know not what oClock it is but the children are all in bed) I hope we shall be sitting together— I guess you will leave Hindwell about the Wednesday, therefore in all likelihood this will be the last letter I shall send thither for you, but in this I shall be guided by what you say in your next— I was rejoiced to have such good accounts of Saras & Joanna's looks but you do not mention dear Tom. I hope he looked well also & dear Mary— give my best Love to them all & tell them that I have many a longing to see them all together — but I cannot forgive them for going so far from us. — this feeling presses harder upon me at times than any of them has an idea of— 15 years! Good luck, we dispose of ourselves as if this world were for ever— Well! next Saturday but one & *we* meet to part no more for any length of time— till

---

[4]Mary wrote "forthnight."

a sod separates us, & that separation I trust will be for no great length of time. O William— but I can not, I *must* not give way to the *movements* of my thoughts— but [? let] me look back to the one that thus led me from speaking of the blessed bond that binds husband & wife so much closer than the bond of Brotherhood— however dear & affectionate a family of Brothers [?&] Sisters may love each other. —

I am sitting in thy study— the rain beats against the window — the fire is flapping & the Baby in the Cradle upon the Sofa, nestling about warning me that he will presently awake, but all these quiet sounds are disturbed by a restless, noisy, chirping, dying (I am afraid) chick that is within the Fender & which the children left to *my* care therefore I have not the heart to dismiss it— it is one of 4 that has been destroyed by the late wet weather— they are, of the younger brood at first 14 in number— The *first* set, of 10, are all alive— they were chipped in a fine season & are able to stand against this change, but John who is the manager is too ready to trust to a sunny gleam & too lazy, or too absent to remember to put them up in time— but *I must* say that his tender heart, gets the better, generally, of his lazyness & watching these young ones is consequently good employment for him. — You will love these little Chicken for the children['s] sake & you will love to see how pretty they look moving amongst the grass & shrubs— Dorothy when I came in was in such an extacy to give me the account of how they had revived this poor thing & made it eat & chirp, *after it had been dead* & poor thing they have made it eat, for its poor crop is the biggest part about it. — I shall leave the scrap unwritten till the Morning for H. & M. are come in so good night my best beloved.—

Sun. Morn^g— Owing to a mistake Sarah's father is come *to-day* with [   ] horse for us all to go to Hacket — we had sent a message which they had [not] received that it was not to be this week— but as they have provided a di[nner] (this we did not intend, but to have *carried* our dinner) for us we must g[o] [   ] [w]hining Tom we must leave at Gannys as he has no father to walk with— [   ] for your being at home for thy

dear Boy's sake he wants attention sadly— [   ] I have had
a letter from D. with [   ] of her journey *upon* the Coach
[   ]! Heaven bless thee my Love

M.W.

Sarah stays with us

6

William to Mary, 19 August 1810

In William's final letter to Mary from Hindwell in 1810, some topics have become familiar; others are fresh, among them news about Mary's bachelor uncle, Henry Hutchinson of Stockton, apparently somewhat of a curmudgeon. When he died in his late seventies the following January, he left Mary and her sister Joanna a farm in Yorkshire valued at £3,000 to £4,000 and then renting at £100 a year; letters of 1812 disclose that he remembered other heirs less generously.

Henry Addison, now farming in Wales, was the brother of Richard Addison, partner at law of Richard Wordsworth. The Stephenses were neighbors at Hindwell. Francis Donaldson soon became a neighbor, leasing Penfunnon farm from Mrs. Ann Stephens. Two summers later when he visited his uncle's farm, Tommy Wordsworth made the Donaldson girls his playmates. William Taylor, a friend of the Hutchinsons, farmed in Durham. James Watt, the engineer famous for his development of the steam engine, owned land in Radnorshire and Breconshire; he often spent holidays at his country home at Doldowlod on the Wye.

William outlined a short tour that retraced a leg of an earlier journey in Wales, when he met the character that inspired *Peter Bell*; he wrote the poem in 1798 and after extensive revisions finally published it in 1819.

Among the voluntary seamstresses stitching clothes for the growing Wordsworth children, the only unfamiliar name is that of Frances Willes Fermor, the widowed sister of Margaret Willes Beaumont, wife of Sir George. William's mysterious "enigma" about an article of apparel with which he intended to surprise Mary remains a lover's secret.

[*84*]

My dearest Love,

Yesterday brought me your 2nd Letter and one from dear Dorothy, informing me of her arrival at Bury after a not unpleasant journey— I was most happy in the sight of both these Letters, particularly of yours as I had not expected quite so confidently, and had been not a little mortified by a sentence in your Letter to Sara in which you had said that you did not intend to write to me till you heard of my arrival here; which expression sadly clouded my prospect of hearing from you twice a week during my stay at Hindwell, as I had desired, & fear[l]essly expected. —

I will begin with noticing the news part of your last. I need not say how much I am mortified at the folly of the girls leaving you particularly Sara— Fanny I could have excused. But I hope we shall be able to suit ourselves as well, and that Dorothy need not return home sooner on account of any uncertainty on this Head. For, I believe I did not tell you, that I suggested to her the idea of staying longer, on Mrs Montagu's account; whom I so exceedingly despise that I did not wish that D— who has never seen her, should have that disagreeable business to encounter. I talked with D— on this head and she was in sympathy with me. To Montagu I shall behave most kindly as my mind will prompt, but to his partner with nothing more than civility. In fact the Creature is utterly odious to me. I have, however, the satisfaction of foreseeing that we shall not be troubled long with their company as she will be for jaunting off to Keswick to see Southey &c, and C—[1] who I hope will not be returned. — I cannot say my Love with what fondness I feed on the thought of our being together without interruption day or night. I am indeed, on many accounts sorely vexed at this visit from the M's, but far above all as it will interfere with our solitudes, so happily given, and so long and often desired. — But my heart is leading me aside when I meant only to speak for a while of matters of fact. — I do not like Gawens

[1]Coleridge.

[85]

Hindwell, with its pool in the foreground, Radnorshire, Wales; photographed by Thomas Stephens, c. 1880. Collection of Jenny Dainty.

conduct about the School, but I shall not be in a hurry to interfere; at all events we must come to some resolution about John. As to the parsonage there are doubtless many and great objections, and we shall decide upon it within a week after my return at latest, as we will not be trifled with. — Yesterday Tom had a Letter from Jack 3 days later date than that to you in which he says that your Uncle is weak, and that he has lately remade his will, and, as he told Jack in the best disposition to *you* all. Jack adds, that he has left you a piece of land. So I suppose he knows thoroughly how things are disposed of.— —

The weather since I came here saving these two last days has been rainy and uncomfortable; so that we have only made very short excursions in the neighborhood—. It is a Country of many Vales, this in which Hindwell stands, the longest & widest; but the narrowest vales and the narrow parts of the wide ones are the most pleasing portions of the country. Hindwell House stands very pleasantly however, on account of the Pool in front, & the Hill opposite crowned by old Radnor church, a much more picturesque building than[2] that upon Breadon Hill not far from Coleorton; I have said that Hindwell stands pleasantly *however*, because it stands in a part where the Vale is more than three miles across and comparatively naked, large fields and poor Hedgerows; but the view from the windows is truly delightful, and shews beautifully the great importance of still water in Landscape. By moonlight and in the evening this Pool of three acres, seen from the window with its reflection is little less interesting than[3] one of our Lakes. I have been but a remiss Angler in it but yesterday I caught a very nice fry, eleven, several of them more than half a Pound a piece. I had only tried twice before, and not more than a few minutes, without success.—

The day before yesterday Mary Monkhouse Sara & I rode to Kington after dinner, Sara was seized with a sickness at Kington, and they were obliged to return in a post chaise. — This sickness was caused by a little precipitation in setting off at a time when S— ought to have attended leisurely to a call of Nature— I mention this awkward cause in order that the fact which I could not conceal, might not appear more alarming than it need. She was however, very ill at the time; as to complexion &c as bad as Dorothy in one of her worst fits— She is at present quite well, and I think her complexion is now as good as it was before. Yester evening Mary M—[4] & Joanna H. Addison & I walked and I was very sorry to find that the walking up hill brought a pain into M.M's side. She is by no means strong, and requires being treated with care. Long and laborious walks ought to be avoided by all means. Her digestion is bad and she is very thin; but it is a most favorable circumstance that she will here have every advantage for taking Horse exer-

[2]William wrote "that."
[3]William wrote "that."
[4]Monkhouse.

cise, the best thing in the world for her— Joanna and she & John M—[5] are ridden out (this Afternoon (Sunday) to drink tea at one of the Stephens's (not the Lover) two miles and a half off. — To Morrow I go with Tom & a Mr Donaldson who is here to view a Farm 12 miles off, towards Leominster, which Mr D— has some thoughts of taking. Mr D— was formerly a Barrister, a Friend of W. Taylors, with whom & at St Helens he has been 3 years to learn the craft of a Farmer— He is a mild good natured little man, of humble desires, but I much fear that humble as his desires are he will not find it easy to gratify them in the farming line; which as far as profit is concerned seems but a poor speculation. Mr D— was yesterday with Tom to look at a farm upon the Wye, belonging to James Watt of Birmingham. It is small, about 120 acres, and enchantingly situated in both which particulars it would suit Mr D— but I do not think there is much likelihood of its being let reasonably— —

I shall attempt during the course of the next week to make a short tour upon the Wye with some part of the family Sara if possible. If you will look at the Map you will see the course I purpose to take. from Radnor new or old to the Hay upon the Wye, thence to Bualth, in which road long ago I met the original of Peter Bell, thence up the Wye to Rhaiader, I doubt whether I spell right, and then across the country again to Radnor which is two miles from this place. This excursion with the peeps into the valleys on the side of the Wye, I mean tributary to it will take from three to 4 days. I have not yet spoken to Sara of the length of my intended stay here but I am sure she will be very good in letting me take my departure, as she knows and cannot but feel for your loneliness, and knows also though she cannot feel that how my Beloved longs for my return. Your last Letter I gave her to read both for her own gratification & that she might be awakened in some degree by it to a sense of this longing. Your former Letter I kept to my self and only read her such parts as related to matter of fact. The general strain of it was too sacred and too intensely connubial for any eye but my own—

[5]Monkhouse.

And now my sweet and dearest love I am brought to the point where I may allow my heart to flow over a little, and but a little. But first let me tell the news about my eye which will tend to brighten what I have to say of love and hope and joy, it is, indeed at last considerably better, though still liable to derangement upon slight causes, and the swelling is far from being abated, though the inflammation is; but in fact after the inflammation is gone a relaxation is left behind which is very slow to disappear, and which I am inclined to think never goes away wholly. The eyelid, however, is not now, strikingly unsightly, which it was from the size of the inflammation, all the while I was at Coleorton—. I am thankful that it is better, as I am sure it would have been some time before but for the cause I mentioned, which has always intervened till lately to throw it back. But the prospect of seeing my Beloved again so soon makes me more tranquil both day & night, at least enables me better to bear my longings, and to keep more genially and comfortably. My darling, I hope, we shall not part again speedily! What happiness did that part of thy Letter give me in which thou speaks of the Compliments received upon thy good looks— Let me here exact a promise from thee, that when thou hast reason to expect me, thou wilt not fail to put on that Cap in which by thy own confession thou lookest best; in order that I may see thee with as much promise of health and comeliness and long life Upon thy sweet countenance as heaven will allow. I have some other promises to exact from thee but these I reserve till we meet, though I will let thee into them so far as not to leave it unsaid that they are of the same kind. And here let me not forget to add that I will bring thee a Bonnet from Liverpool; a Gypsey one Joanna recommends, and such it shall be if I can please myself, or rather if I think I can please thee; but I have not forgotten the Penrith gown; this remembrance, however, shall not cause me to despair, but only rouze me to a more careful and deliberate choice. — By the bye, who are the fine folks at the Church stile? — who presume to look insolently upon thee with our little William in thy arms? — Sara & M. M have been busy in making frocks for little Catharine & D— so that with what I shall bring and Mrs Fermors, I hope, they will be provided for sometime.

I have but a little space on this private side of the sheet to sigh for thee and tell thee, that I am giddy at the thought of seeing thee once more, to tell thee also that those parts of my day are in my thoughts a thanksgiving to God for having blessed an unworthy Creature as I am with such a treasure, as thy gentle, thy loving, thy faithful thy pure spirit; for having united us by the sacred bond of husband and wife, and for having bound us still more closely together by those sweet darlings whose images pass and repass across my mind all day long like the clouds in the firmament. Above all dear little Catharine I think of most for her infirmity's sake, and her little pretty ways— Kiss her for her fathers sake, and kiss them all— What shall I bring them, what shall I bring John, has puzzled me most. If my promise should be fulfilled, the promise I mean I have made to my self I shall be home this day fortnight; and yet I think it is scarcely possible, when I bear in mind that I must be at least 4 days on the road. Be assured however that I shall do my utmost, and if any thing takes place to prevent me, you shall be apprized. I dare scarcely promise it now, that the time is so much nearer; but it will partly depend upon the length of this little Tour (which I think will leave a more lively remembrance of my having been here on Sara's mind than any thing else) and upon the time when we set off upon it: be assured that I will do my utmost to be with you, consistently with what I owe to others; and, knowing this, expect me with chearfulness and if you can with tranquillity. — I am rather hurt, on Mr Wilsons account that he has not been able to find time to pay you a moments visit, but he is a strange irregular Creature.—

I have written the greatest part of this Letter by Candlelight,[6] and I do not feel that my eyes have suffered, but I expect to be called every moment to supper, so that I am pleased to have got so far before I was interrupted. I do not expect to hear from you to morrow, nor from Dorothy and therefore I am little anxious about the post; & should not be in the smallest degree so if I were quite assured, which I never can be that I

---

[6]William wrote "Candlenight."

shall hear from neither of you. Your B^r Tom seems a good deal pleased with H. Addison and thinks it likely that he will prove an attentive Farmer: indeed he seems a[7] very obliging and amiable young Man, of moderate desires, and likely to be as happy as a man whose life is not intellectual can be; I mean if his health should prove good. I have left no room for Sara, or any Body; S— seems upon very good reasons determined against Miss Weir for Betsy, but no doubt in a day or two she will write herself— I have not read this Letter so excuse all blunders and fill up omissions by your own ingenuity. farewell, my dear Wife, and beloved Mary.

W W.

I must again bid thee farewell on this side of the Paper with a thousand kisses 1000.

Try, Love, to guess my Enigma about promises connected with the subject of dress, it was often entreated, by me but I could never prevail upon thee) to accord me that indulgence.— again farewell.

[7] William wrote "an."

Mary to William, 24–25 August 1810

This letter concludes William and Mary's correspondence of 1810. She was eager, as she wrote, to ascertain the day of his return. But because the correspondents laid down their pens, we cannot know the precise date on which William panted up the hill to Allan Bank, held Mary in his arms once more, and delivered presents to excited children; and we are left to imagine how he was shown—proudly—Catharine's new teeth, the chicks that had hatched at the drawing-room fender, and the fine crop of hay, whose harvest Mary had overseen. With the family reunion, a curtain was drawn.

Aggy (Agnes) Ashburner was the daughter of Peggy and Thomas Ashburner of Townend, Grasmere. William Enfield's *Speaker*, first published in 1774 and frequently reprinted, was a popular book on elocution.

Friday Even^g Aug. 24th.

My dearest Love

I am grieved to the heart that I did not forward a letter to you about the middle of the week, as I am led to think from what you say in the letter which I hold in my hand that you would look for one from me written at that time— & I was much inclined to do so, but as I was confidently expecting *your* letter to reach me before now, I put off writing in order that I might have the satisfaction of speaking of it— You have neglected to date *this* letter, which was a great oversight, as you date the time of your probable absence from the day upon which you write— your former letter was written on a Saturday & it came by Wednesday's post this by Friday's— Yet I cannot but think that *this* was written on Saturday likewise, because you say this day 3 weeks in the one, & this day fortnight in the other— without mentioning that you have departed from your intention— Yet I do not positively expect you so soon as tomorrow week, anxious as I am to have you here, therefore I shall send off this letter to Hindwell, — had I been *confident* I should have directed to Mr Crump's— I am most happy in the account you give me of the improvement in your health & state of your feelings,— I trust my beloved! you will come to me looking well, & unfatigued— that you may not require a few days to *bring yourself round* for in that case the Montagu's will be upon us before we have had time first to feel our happiness at home— by our own fire side. & afterwards to enjoy, if the weather will favour us long half-day rambles about, or out of the Vale— My little Darling need never prevent this— if you come, strong enough & with spirits to lead you into the woods & fields— I am become so well able to nurse, by being accustomed to it that, I carry this little fellow about with me just as we used to do John, & with as much or more ease & he is a child that you may do what you please with.— such a Sleeper! & such a Thriver! — He is to be cut for the small pox on Sunday (the matter to be taken from a child of Astley's Brother in Law, who lives in R. Newton's house with his Wife & 3 children & 3 Servants as I told you before, besides many other things which I find from D.[1] you have not heard of— which convinces me that some of my letters must have been lost) the *small pox* is in the Vale— a Boy at the Miller's is dangerously ill in them & they cannot make out how he caught the infection— — This poor Vale is a harbour for all ill things at present— Tom Wilson is rubbing for the itch, & what do you think of a Massy stately gateway an entrance into, & a second road (a Coach road) thro' that beautiful field at Tail end— this gateway is seen plainly

[1]Dorothy Wordsworth.

from the high road and the house, which was before a pretty one, connected with it is become an abominable impertinence— these things vex me far more that you are absent than if you were here to share the vexation with me— The Sale of Butterlip how which I wonder you do not mention is either to be upon the 11th. or 13th. of next Month. But let me turn to your letter which I received a while ago at the Town-end where I had been waiting for it for nearly 2 hours—

God in heaven bless thee for sending me such nice long letters, with such blessed intelligence! — but what you say of dear Sara's Sickness has thrown a cruel damp over me— she must have been very ill indeed to submit to be put into a chaise— I wish you had said there was *no blood* thrown off her stomach— yet I trust that if there had been, you *would* have said so— your being doubtful which of them was to accompany you on your intended tour frightened me— I hope I shall have another letter from you, if not one from herself also, in a day or two— tomorrow I shall examine the Map & trace where you have been, for I suppose you have returned to Hindwell by this time— & tomorrow *morning* I must finish my letter in order not to miss Sunday's Post— I must now be forced to leave off to take my supper my little Man having slept all the Evening & most of the forenoon wants me to go to bed— it is about 11 oClock— I will just tell you what has been the subject of conversation at Town end lest I forget in the Morning— Poor Aggy Ashburner is in the same situation as her sisters without having any hope of being made an honest woman of— Peggy is as you may suppose distracted— & Thos. who I am most sorry for is quite depressed— As to Aggy's self she has I find little feeling about it— she is, which I never knew before, only a half-wit— poor Soul very much like our Betsy— But good night my blessing! the baby cries— which is most unusual but he is about his teeth— C.[2] really is almost well— —

Sat. Morning I must try thro' many interruptions to finish my letter— I find upon re-reading yours that it was written last

[2] Catharine Wordsworth.

Sunday— so I hope this will not be too late, even if you keep to the time you propose to yourself to leave Hindwell— The weather now is delightful— Yesterday I think was the hottest day we have had & this is a lovely morning— I think, surely the greatest part of the hay will be housed to night— Mr King finished yesterday. I do look upon myself to be the *best Manager,* in spite of difficulties in the Vale— — The children have all been about me during breakfast, nursing a dying chicken again— You would have been entertained to have heard the wishes they uttered for Hartleys arrival, whom they look upon to be infallible— one having recovered under his direction last week— but he is come & this poor thing will die in spite of him— to be sure he told them upon learning that the Cock had pecked it— that he was not a "proficient in cases of surgery— it was only internal diseases that he understood"— he is wonderfully good natured with them for they almost tease his life out, to go to assist them with these Chicken (3 *pair* as Sissy says they have, meaning 3 *Sets*) & he cannot refuse, tho' he takes his hat & hurrys out quite in a passion— he says they are *terrible Children* for such things, for they never let him rest either about the Calf the Pig or something & he is not "adapted to the business of a farm yard"— We have heard nothing of Derwent this week— The Lasses have come to their senses & have consented to keep their places— I have hired them for a year & they are to have each a Guinea more wages— We had a very delightful day at Hacket last Sunday & the Children all enjoyed themselves— poor Toms absence I lamented— but he spent his day most happily at the Carrier's preferring to stay there to either of the other two houses— Pray do not look coolly upon M.D.[3] when you return, for I believe she has been heartily sorry for having refused to come to me & has done all she could to make it up— it is never worth while taking any notice of it— Dear Dorothy! I was quite hurt to think of her being obliged to mount on the top of a Coach alone, at 12 oClock at night— & I cannot forgive the Beaumonts for leaving her to risk such a thing,— why was she not seen into the *Cambridge* Coach by

---

[3] Mary Dawson.

some one of the Family? when it was to be taken no farther from them than at Leicester— — What a transition for her— from the luxuries of Coleorton Hall! — She seems determined not to return to meet the Montagu's & I think she is right— & I hope she will return by Stockton, only the expences frighten me— she tells me that money goes very fast with her,— I know not how we are to stand all this out, for I have never heard that Lady B. has born any part in it— Tell Joanna that a Gypsey Hat does not suit me as it used to do, now that I always wear a Cap & am cropped— I should best like a large close Bonnet— but I think thou must drop the thought of getting me one, as I do not see what thou couldst bring, except a straw Bonnet & those cost so much money, & are not very serviceable, & we *so poor* that I must een try to do without one this year. —

Thomas Ashburner makes me boggle about Butterlip how— (he is sure that Mr J.[4] will lose a deal of money by it, as we understand it is *positively* to be sold) for he says that if Mr King bid 1200[5] for it he far outbid its worth. It is to be sold at Mr Wilcock's— If you do not come about the end of this week I fear you may miss Mr Crump, as he is expected to be at the Assizes— probably he may be here very soon, for the Regatta at Ambleside is on Monday & tuesday next— I pray that no accidents may happen, for You never heard what foolish work is to go forward & expensive work too— I am grieved for Mr Wilson— You still say nothing why Mr Blair was not with you—. I cannot help you to determine what your presents to the Children must be— they are at a loss themselves— Mr de Q.[6] sent John word that *his Artillery* was packed up— (I suppose the present had been previously settled between them) but he can not think of any thing for you to bring but a book, poor fellow little use as books are of to him, & *Enfield's Speaker* is the one he most inclines to— I am very glad about the frocks for they want new ones sadly— & tell Tom that if he has an old Coat & you room in your Trunk I will thank him to send John one— he need not fear about *its badness* when I tell you that I have

[4]Jackson.
[5]Mary wrote "12–00."
[6]De Quincey.

made a handsome jacket & Waistcoat out of your Blue Jacket!
— I do not forget that they have a little Lad of their own, but
as there are 3 of them who will all cast better coats than you do;
I think it is possible they may spare one. Pray remember *all* my
messages to Mr Crump— & let the oil & Rice be sent as soon as
possible, the oil particularly— Indeed my Love I cannot find
out thy Enigma, for I cannot possibly recollect your ever in-
treating any thing of me connected with the subject of dress—
if *dress had been entirely out of the question* I might have made a
guess. —

And now I think I have answered circumstantially the whole
of your letter & having told you that we are all remarkably well
Catharine improving fast (this muffle on her hand has done
much good) though she looks ill, being still struggling with her
teeth— I shall after dressing her poor sore finger go out to
endeavour to send off my letter,— reserving all further communion (not without a reason for so doing) till we meet, unless
I hear that your stay is prolonged, or you fix a time for a letter
to meet you at Mr Crump's— for which happy time I shall wait
in joyful expectation— as the time draws near I shall dread a
disappointment— but do not leave them abruptly, or if any
thing you wish to see, prompts you to delay our meeting for a
few days even, do not let your anxiety to be at home, or fear of
disappointing me prevent this— for I will prepare myself to
expect such a thing— & it may be we may not afterwards regret this privation— particularly if your keeping to your time is
to cost much pain to others, give it up— for a short while
longer.

Farewell my best beloved, above all be good to thyself— &
this is the best thou canst do for us all who love thee— I have
looked upon the Map, but the only name you have given me
that I have yet found out is Hay— I shall after I have forwarded my letter look more leisurely— if you are out to day I
hope you will have a perfect enjoyment of all you see & feel,
for it is a day made on purpose for you— oh would I were
travelling by your side— next Summer if we are richer we must
manage something of this sort & I think our journey must be
into Wales, for I am sure I shall grow most restless to see Tom

& Joanna before next Summer is over & dear Mary M. also—
& I have not heard of any one thing in Scotland that I have
such a desire to see, as I have to travel along the banks of the
Wye— God eternally bless you all! & thee my Love may he
send to me safely & well, then shall I be the most happy &
blessed Wife in the World— Tell Sara that the bairns talk far
more about their Aunt Sara's coming home again than they do
about either your return or their Aunt's—[7] God love you again
& again

[7]Dorothy Wordsworth.

8

Mary to William, 23 April 1812

Fortune did not disrupt the rhythm of the Wordsworths' lives between the autumn of 1810 and the spring of 1812, but the period could hardly be called uneventful. The children hacked, rasped, and vomited for months with tenacious cases of whooping cough, and death seemed imminent for Catharine. When Dorothy returned from her travels in late October 1810, she alleged that she "never saw so deplorable an object" as Catharine, "worn to a skeleton," unable to "make her voice heard above a faint whisper," or "to lift up her eyes" (*MY*, I, 440). But the little ones weathered the siege. Fear of contagion by scarlet fever in Grasmere led the family to harbor—safely—at John Wilson's home in Windermere for six weeks. Johnny was scalded, Tommy got worms, Willy caught the chickenpox, and Sarah Youdell and Fanny Turner, the servants, came down with debilitating fevers.

But little Willy learned to walk. "William stumps about the floor most stoutly," his father reported, "and with his broad chest and his round bonnet turned up on one side looks not unlike Henry the 8th" (*MY*, I, 509). Playtime gave way to hours in the classroom, and the adults in the family helped out in the village school. The youngsters, however, made only halfhearted scholars. "Poor John's Duncery is intolerable," Dorothy lamented (*MY*, I, 449). Gastrointestinal disorders and eye troubles harassed William, but he composed a cluster of political sonnets and substantial sections of his long philosophical poem, *The Excursion*. Mary gained strength and "looks better than ever she did in her life," Dorothy affirmed at the end of 1810. "She is grown fat and lusty" (*MY*, I, 460).

Late in the spring of 1811 the family moved from Allan Bank to the old Rectory in Grasmere, renovated for their tenancy. But, situated on an undrainable bog, it too proved cold and damp, and again the chimney in the sitting room smoked so badly that no fires could be lit there. Nonetheless, the family was delighted to be able to remain in Grasmere—the valley "sweeter than paradise itself," Dorothy avowed (*MY*, I, 406)—for houses of the size they required were hard to come by.

Mary's old uncle Henry Hutchinson died in January 1811, leaving her a small legacy, but money became a problem as family expenses grew right along with the children. Before the move to the Rectory, Dorothy divulged, "We intend to give over drinking tea, and if possible, to take a house where coals are cheaper" (*MY*, I, 385). And William complained, "Postage oppresses me, in our present poverty" (*MY*, I, 515). Early in 1812 Wordsworth wrote to Lord Lonsdale, the Earl of Lowther, requesting his assistance in securing a minor government appointment that would relieve the family finances. While Lonsdale was unable to help at the time, in 1813 he used his influence to obtain for Wordsworth the distributorship of stamps for Westmorland and part of Cumberland. (Wordsworth's responsibility then was to supervise the collection of inland revenue duties.)

Yet another problem distressed the Wordsworths during these months: Coleridge. For many years they had loved him as a brother, but his illness made friendship taxing and difficult. When he shared their home at Allan Bank, he often rose in the afternoon, required special food, and lied about what he had written. The opium he had begun to take as an anodyne became an isolating addiction, but his sincerest attempts to renounce it failed. In October 1810, when the Montagus visited the Lake Country, Basil offered Coleridge a home with them in London and recommended medical treatment. So that Montagu would be fully aware of Coleridge's habits and condition and because William believed the scheme doomed, he warned Montagu of the behavior he might expect of Coleridge and recounted experiences that had grieved the Wordsworths during his sojourn at Allan Bank. William intended to counsel Coleridge against the design as well—Coleridge had never cared much for Montagu and the plan was conceived in haste—but they set off for London before William found an opportunity. En route Montagu foolishly repeated William's caveat to Coleridge, suggesting that Wordsworth had commissioned him to do so. Hurt and angry, Coleridge immediately broke with Montagu. He sent no reproach to William, however, allowing his wounds to fester while complaining bitterly elsewhere of ill usage. The Wordsworths were accustomed to Coleridge's silences and failed to realize that anything was amiss until the following spring. Slowly they pieced together the history of the misunderstanding and appealed to friends to encourage Coleridge to communicate with them. They did not approach him directly, and, bruised and proud, he declined to make the first move. The Wordsworths remained confident that they would see him when he next came north, but that hope collapsed in February 1812, when Coleridge drove past their door without stopping, as Hartley sat speechless with astonishment beside him in the chaise and Derwent's eyes glistened with tears. Coleridge returned to London at the end of March, having made no gesture of friendship. A fortnight later William followed him, determined to confront Montagu and resolve the unhappy dilemma. The matter was finally settled on 11 May, when an explanatory letter from Wordsworth mollified Coleridge.

Two years earlier William had vowed that he would never part from Mary for more than a week or two unless "compelled by a sense of duty that leaves no choice." The misunderstanding with Coleridge seems to have forged the spur. Mary shared her husband's reluctance to be separated, but she had little taste for London life and had long looked forward to a visit with her brother in Wales. Although William apparently undertook his excursion as a duty and deplored the excesses of the Regency beau monde in which he made his debut, there is a zest in his reports to Mary that suggests genuine exhilaration. His circle of acquaintances widened, and he found himself courted and pursued—a man whose achievements were honored and whose opinions mattered. As we watch him attend parliamentary debates and talk politics with eminent statesmen, we cannot help wondering whether Wordsworth considered standing for Parliament in 1812. If so, this dutiful journey to London was also a testing, an investigation of the political sphere.

William, Mary, and Tommy Wordsworth left the Rectory on 12 April, journeying together to Chester, where Mary's brother Tom met them. Tom Hutchinson escorted Mary and his namesake (often referred to by his pet name, Totts) to Hindwell, where his sister Joanna, cousins Mary and John Monkhouse, aunt Elizabeth Monkhouse, and, shortly, brother George were also in residence. William proceeded south alone. At Grasmere Dorothy Wordsworth and Sara Hutchinson remained in command of a much diminished household. Dora Wordsworth was away at school.

Like William, Mary was an indefatigable sightseer. Here, looking forward to viewing the lovely scenery surrounding the river Wye, which Wordsworth described so evocatively in his *Lines Written a Few Miles above Tintern Abbey* (1798), Mary mistook the Dee for the Wye; she corrected her error in her next letter. The Frenchmen Mary observed were prisoners of war, captured in Spain. The French "friend" was the officer Eustace Baudouin, an acquaintance of Annette Vallon, held at Oswestry, in Shropshire. Wordsworth appears to have made efforts toward his release. Four years later Wordsworth's French daughter, Caroline, married Baudouin's older brother, Jean-Baptiste Martin Baudouin.

Joanna Hutchinson's prediction of the marriage of Tom Hutchinson and his cousin Mary Monkhouse was fulfilled in Grasmere the following November. George Hutchinson, the family's black sheep, had left his post on a Lincolnshire farm and sought a new position. George and Henry Hutchinson, Mary's sailor brother, inherited very small bequests from old Henry Hutchinson, whereas Tom and John (Jack) received bountiful legacies. The business to be settled with the executors was the signing of new deeds of title.

William's "good cousin" was William Cookson, at Brasenose College, Oxford, son of the Reverend William Cookson, Wordsworth's uncle, canon of Windsor and rector of Binfield. Wordsworth had supper with his cousin, but as the young man was indisposed with a severe cough and cold, the poet was probably spared most of the chatter Mary had feared. "Johnsy" was the Reverend William Johnson, recently curate and schoolmaster at Grasmere. He went to London earlier in the year to become headmaster of the new National School. He was writing primers for schoolchildren in the spring, on one of which Wordsworth agreed to collaborate. Orlande is unidentified.

Hindwell April 23^d. Thursday Morn^g
My dearest Love
   I know thou wilt be anxious to meet with intelligence from us upon thy arrival in London— I therefore prefer writing a short letter by to days post to running the risk of your having to wait a few days, which might be the case if I deferred sending a letter till Saturday— By that time I hope I shall hear from you & pray that you may have as good an account for me, of y[our]-self & of your journey as I have to give you. —
   I think you seemed better at our parting, & I wished you might not suffer yourself to be wearied with listening to the Chatter of your good Cousin— however as the early departure of the Coach furnished you with a good excuse for retiring soon, I think you would take advantage of it and get early to bed. I will now tell you briefly *our* progress, saving all particulars till we meet— as you would expect, we reached Wrexam before dark— the afternoon was delightful & I was (notwithstanding a sad damp oppressed me when I felt myself travelling in a contrary direction to thee my best Darling!) much pleased with my ride— we turned aside to look at the prospect Mr Crump pointed out to Sarah near the beautiful church with the Yew trees, & saw into a rich bottom, but were not certain that we saw what had been recommended, for there was no river in the view from the point we could conveniently come at in the Gig, & I did not at that time much like getting in and out, not being accustomed to the Mare— afterwards, I did not mind this, when I understood her ways, & was without fear all the rest of the journey— on Sunday Morning we walked round the Wrexam Church & into it— & then had a most heavenly ride to Oswestry where we dined Oh with what a fervent heart did I greet the river Wye for thy sake & for its own loveliness!— I looked for our friend in the face of every Frenchman we met, & never before was sorry that I could not speak their language I was sorry for his sake that you had not come so far with us— for I dare say he has never rec^d. his father's [   ]

letters. At Welshpool too I could not but be interested for those poor Men— here we slept, Tom had a bad bed & has gotten a cold upon his chest— In the morning we saw the gorgeous Castle of Powis— & much were we all delighted little Tom not the least so— what glorious Evergreens!— a winter Garden is a delightful thing, & this is well suited to its situation— You have seen it have you not? Terrace above Terrace. — The *Kings* bed & the curious cabinets were great treats to Tom— but he did not much like the painted stair case— he could not conceive why the men were all *so bloody*— he shewed great discrimination & was most curious about the *ages* of the Statues Pictures &c— Powis Castle is indeed a fine situation— & the grounds are very interesting— there is no trimness beyond the Garden— & indeed none appears there. the Shrubs are now so very large & flourishing & I never saw any thing like the Ivy. the berries were hanging in such profuse clusters nearly as large as Grapes— we sauntered a very long time here— consequently made a bad day's work as far as our journey was considered— dined & walked about the Castle &c at Montgomery a place I was well pleased with & slept at Bishop's Castle— we *bated* next morn^g at Knighton & reached Hindwell about 4 oClock found all well— No journey could have been more prosperous than this has been— nothing but fine weather— we had a hail shower within the few last miles— but for this the same bright sunshine the whole way. — I enjoyed it for thee as well as for ourselves— but I *do* hope that you did not travel on the top of the Coach. I would give a great deal to know where you are now—

Hindwell is very much like what I [ex]pected & yet very different— but it is a [pre]tty place & I hope to enjoy it thoroughly— [   ] that I am to see you here— by the bye [let] me tell you before I turn to the other side of the paper that Joanna seems certain (& I see nothing to make me doubt that her suspicions are not accurate) that T. & M. M.[1] will soon be married— she thinks the scheme is, that this is to take place at

[1]Tom Hutchinson and Mary Monkhouse.

Grasmere in the Autumn— Of course you must not name this— as the parties have never told her so— but Mary does not deny the main fact— when Joanna taxes her with it. For my part if Mary's health was re-established I should rejoice in it— but I shall not be curious to find out that it is so— Mary looks better than I expected to see her— I wrote in haste to Grasmere yesterday & forgot to mention to Sarah[2] about her intention of being so much away while you were absent I wish you would advise about it if you have not written— Pray my Love write as soon as you can to George & if possible enquire for a place for him & do direct his attention to another place in preference to a farm— Tom met with a letter at home from John wishing him to go to Stockton about signing the deeds & settling the business with the Executors— as the papers he says are of too much value to send so far— Tom thinks this a needless errand— the subject of H & G.[3] was not named in the letter— *this business might* be a reason for his going, but the *time* does not suit Tom, he has written to John to day & I hope made the proposal I recommended— but it will be of no avail I believe. Most likely T. wishes to defer the journey till *other business* calls him to the North. — Remember to send George's letter to Grasmere. Say Totts has been the best Traveller in the world & is very well— but I fear there will be a stand in his learning— he wants the stimulant of his Class fellows & his attention is so much diverted— we have had a serious quarrel this mor^g— which I hope may be beneficial— they are all delighted with him & he *is* a sweet fellow— I shall say nothing about leaving him so do you not name it,— but shall be guided by circumstances— My best Love to Chris & his family & the Beaumonts & most particularly to *Johnsy*— [p]ray send us one of his books & some money as soon as [yo]u can— for I had flannel Petticoats & other ne[cessities to] purchase & I do not like to be obliged to ask T[om to le]nd me money when there is no particul[ar reaso]n for it you know you can get a frank— [hea]ven bless

---

[2] Sara Hutchinson.
[3] Henry and George Hutchinson.

thee evermore I am quite well— but [   ] all cried out how old and Ill I looked— the co[ld is] not quite off my chest   thy M.W.

Tom sends you a kiss— I dreamt last night an ugly dream about one of thy teeth dropping out— I long to hear about thee & all thy doings— have you seen or heard of Orlande

9

William to Mary, 29 April 1812

At Windsor William wrote a diary of his recent movements, and sent it to Grasmere with instructions that it be forwarded to Mary. It was slow in reaching her, and William's apparent silence caused her some uneasiness. He described mounting the coach at Chester on a Sunday morning at four o'clock: "The frost was very severe but the birds were chaunting their love songs careless of the cold, and the sun rose in splendour." At Birmingham he called on the senior Lloyds, then pressed on to Stratford-upon-Avon, and, admiring the countryside, he concluded that Shakespeare had been "fortunate in his birthplace." He found Oxford an "enchanting place," visited his cousin William Cookson, saw the "Curiosities," and chanced to witness John Taylor Coleridge, nephew of the poet, perform brilliantly in a *viva voce* éxamination. He departed with regret, wishing that he might linger another day. At Windsor William enjoyed his reunion with his aunt, uncle, and cousins—especially Mary, a favorite of his. The Cooksons' eldest son, Christopher, had dropped out of Cambridge after one year of only desultory study.

William replied to Mary's letter from the Beaumonts' house in Grosvenor Square. While she luxuriated in an uncharacteristic repose at Hindwell, William embarked on a hectic round of social activity. After seeking his brother Christopher, he called on Montagu, first at the Inns of Court, where Montagu had rooms, and then at his home. Charles Lamb, renowned as a humorist and essayist, was employed at the East India House. David Wilkie was a popular British painter. Washington Allston, an American artist, had lived in Rome but resided in England from 1811 to 1818. The Reverend Samuel Parr was an educator and author. Charles was Montagu's son by his third marriage; Alfred and William were his sons by his second. Anne Skepper was Mrs. Montagu's daughter by her first marriage.

Taylor, Sir George Beaumont's agent at Coleorton, had been guilty of improper conduct earlier; now Beaumont had dismissed him. William's brother Richard owned a farm at Sockbridge, not far from Grasmere, but the other Wordsworths seldom saw him. "He is a curious brother," Dorothy once remarked, when Richard had been several weeks in the north without making his presence known (*MY*, I, 371). Richard "Conversation" Sharp, writer and West India merchant, sat for Castle Rising in the House of Commons from 1806 to 1812. To save postage William asked friends in parliament to frank letters for him, a common practice at the time. Captain Charles Luff and his wife, Letitia, had been friends of the Wordsworths when the Luffs lived at Patterdale; in the spring of 1812 they set out for Mauritius. Luff had appealed to Wordsworth for a loan of £100, which William refused him, after consultation, as an unsound risk. Mary, Dorothy, and Sara Hutchinson chorused their disappointment at the decision.

Grosvenor
Wednesday April 29th

My beloved Mary, a Letter which about this time you will have received, will have informed you how I fared till Thursday last. My stay at Windsor was longer than I intended, viz, two days; the one, Saturday, I gave as an act of generosity, and the other as I was obliged to give, as it would have been indecent to have left a Clergymans House on a Sunday, without necessity. On Monday at 3 oclock in the afternoon I left Windsor, and reached this place, before 7; and had my Coffee immediately, sitting alone till past 11 when the Beaumonts arrived; both well and looking well. — Nothing could be kinder than the Cooksons; Mary is a sensible Girl; and I think has full as much intellect as any of the brood. Christopher, now gone to

India, appears to have been most foolishly extravagant. I wish, dearest Love, you had as good an appetite as Mrs Cookson; she is deplorably thin, but in good health and spirits. My Uncle wears uncommonly well. — —

I was most happy to find here a Letter from you and one from Dorothy. How ill the poor Lasses have been! I half fear that bog behind & about the Parsonage must be [a] very unwholesome thing and wish we were in another House. Glad am I [to] find you had so pleasant [a] journey; I am sorry that I did not go with you as far as Oswestry; both for the beauty of the scenery, and because I have since heard from my French Friend. He declines at *present* any pecuniary aid; but begs that I would exert myself for his release; with little hope however of success. Yesterday I went to Lambeth; but found that Chris[r] was gone into the Country. He was expected home to day. Pris: has been in the Country 3 weeks; not however I believe at Bocking. Is not this strange? with whom are her Children all this while?— They are a crazy set, those Ll[ds].— I then went to M's[1] Chambers, and finding him not at home proceeded to his House. found them both well— there I dined and spent the evening. I did not break in upon C's[2] business as immediately after dinner M— was summoned to attend a consultation. — I have this morning written to C Lamb begging he would let me know when I shall find him at home and alone; as I wish to have the business sifted to the bottom, and will take his opinion how it may be done in the most unexceptionable manner. —

Time turns to little account in London. I spent all Yesterday morning in my excursion to Lambeth, perspiring about Westminster Hall seeing Wilkies pictures, and another Exhibition, and hunting out Montagu. I have yet seen nobody else. To day I wrote to George. Your account about T. & M—[3] does not surprize me; and should her health be reestablished it will be I think a very desirable Thing. I am pretty confident you have little satisfaction from the application to Jack. — Coleridge

[1] Montagu.
[2] Coleridge.
[3] Tom Hutchinson and Mary Monkhouse.

Grosvenor Square, north side, by Thomas Malton, printed in his *Picturesque Tour through the Cities of London and Westminster* (2 vols., London 1792, 1800). The Beaumonts' town house, number 34 (now demolished), was in the southwest corner of the square, overlooking this view.

called here yesterday at 4 oclock. — I find he has wished to tell his story to the B's[4] with plentiful abuse of me to which they would not listen. This is scandalous conduct on his part, and most ungrateful. Coleridge & Alston dined lately here. Sir G— does not appear to think so highly of the only one of Alstons pictures which he has seen, as I expected. — As to his conversation Lady B— says C— will let nobody talk but himself— I heard an Artist mention Alston yesterday, he says that he thinks he paints too timidly, and would much improve by a continued residence in this Country—

[4]Beaumonts.

Samuel Taylor Coleridge, by Washington Allston, 1814. The National Portrait Gallery, London.

Montagu is superbly lodged, and certainly & wisely denies himself no rational gratification that Money can give. Every accommodation is there in the highest style; and assuredly as far as comfort & liberty go it is impossible to be better than a Man would find himself in their House. Dr Parr is there a pleasant good-humoured old Man; and it will be very convenient and agreeable for me, to call in there when I am not otherwise engaged, even before I take up my residence in the House— — I saw their eldest boy, Charles, a fine and engaging Child. Anne Skepper was there also— Alfred is sent to Bury; and William in order to break the impetuosity of his temper, to a Quaker school; where he is to continue a year or two— a droll Idea this, and truly finical. —

Now, My Love, omit nothing to procure an appetite; for if that be formed, I am sure health and strength will follow. Do not over fatigue thyself. — I am considerably better in health than when I wrote last, but my stomach has not yet recovered its tone if I exceed in eating however little, especially at breakfast, I am oppressed the whole of the day. My misfortune is that my appetite or inclination is no guide for what I ought to eat. — I had no inconvenience from the top of Coach; on the contrary; but still I was more fatigued with my journeys short as they were than I ever remember to have been. — The first night here I slept ill; but last night I made amends. —

I have infinite pleasure in the thought of seeing thee again in Wales; and travelling with thee. — I long for the day. Love me and think of me & wish for me, and be assured that I am repaying thee in the same coin. — It is not to be wondered that Tom's mind is unsettled as to his Book, and that he misses his Companions. Try to encourage him; he is a sweet Boy & will be universally beloved wherever he goes. Write to me frequently & the longest Letters possible; never mind whether you have facts or no to communicate; fill your paper with the breathings of your heart most tenderly your friend & Husband W. W. Love to every one.

Sir G. tells me this affair with Taylor will cost him a thousand Pounds. What a shocking thing besides all the vexation! — Dr

Cookson talks of going down into the North with Mary in the summer time; but I think that he will scarcely accomplish it Richard I shall not see; he is at Sockbridge. I shall speak to Montagu about the Money for Luff. Now mind & write frequent & very very long Letters. Adieu again adieu. W. W. — I shall call on Sharp for Franks —

Of course this Letter does not go to Grasmere I shall write thither to morrow.

10

Mary to William, 2–4 May 1812

Mary received William's first letter from London, but the letter from Windsor sent via Grasmere still had not reached her. Thomas Monkhouse, Mary's cousin and a brother of Mary Monkhouse (M. M.), was a London businessman, best remembered for his later friendship with the poet John Keats. The aunt Mary referred to was Elizabeth Monkhouse. Among the roll of neighbors at Hindwell—Blaxlands, Urwicks, and Stephenses—the Donaldsons' name now appeared. Mr. Donaldson had visited Hindwell while searching for a Welsh farm during William's holiday in 1810, and he later settled at Penfunnon, in Nantmel parish. Tommy recruited Donaldson's daughters Mary and Jessy as playmates. Mary Wordsworth's reading included Richard Allestree's rather pious *The Ladies Calling* (1673) and Gilbert Burnet's popular *History of His Own Time* (1723 and 1734).

An English stone is fourteen pounds. At the weigh-in Mary reported she charted 111 pounds, Mary Monkhouse 108 pounds, Joanna Hutchinson 109 pounds, and little Tom 40 pounds. Mary was no doubt proud to outweigh her competition. Four years earlier Dorothy had declared she was "as thin as I ever saw anybody who could go through the ordinary business of life" and growing "thinner every week" (*MY*, I, 192, 198).

The Wordsworths had ordered a machine to give Catharine electrotherapy treatments for her continuing lameness, but it was never used, as the key to operate it could not be located. Earlier Mary had rubbed Catharine's limbs for two hours a day to help her recover muscular control.

Mary Lamb, writer and sister of Charles Lamb, suffered periodic episodes of insanity. She had killed her mother during one attack and was subsequently confined when she felt the illness approaching. She lived with her brother. John Christian Curwen was a wealthy and influential northern landowner; in 1830 his granddaughter married the Wordsworths' eldest son, John. Annette Vallon was the Frenchwoman with whom William fell in love and whom he intended to marry in 1792. He helped to support their daughter, Caroline.

Hindwell Saturday May 2^d.

My best beloved Friend—

Your letter this morning, from London, has released my mind from the most painful anxiety as you will well suppose when I tell you, that the former letter you speak of, has never reached me— I have been tormented with a thousand fears ever since I have heard the bad accounts from Grasmere, lest you should also be suffering, I knew not where, from the same disease— which I cannot but think with you, is caused by that low & damp situation. & I certainly think it is our duty to get out of the House as soon as we can, having had this warning—

Well my darling Love! I am at last most glad to find thee safely landed in London & tho' the account you give of your health is not the best possible I am satisfied with it in the confidence that thou wilt take good care to manage thyself well, & avoid too much talking— I am grieved that the letter should be lost for your sake as well as my own, as I must beg of you at your leisure to repeat to me how you fared on your journey— perhaps too, you intended *that* letter to be sent to Grasmere, & if so, they will there have been partaking of my fears & anxiety— which would fall heavy upon them in addition to their other troubles— but now thank God I have favorable accounts of them & by this time I trust they are all quite well— Poor dear Dorothy! I have been sorry that she should have been such a Slave. I think you had got a good deal done considering you had been so short a time in Town— but I long to have

further & better accounts from you. I should like you to call upon Tom Monkhouse as soon as you can for Mary's sake. —
Now, my William you will rejoice to hear that I am quite well & have an excellent appetite & now that my mind is at rest about thee I shall be quite happy— We have had a good deal of rain, yet I have been out several times— once I rode behind Tom. M M. single towards Nill— & last thursday we went to dine at Mr Blaxlands, I suppose you know where they live tho' they have come to the neighbourhood since you were here— The day was not very favourable— but I was much pleased with the ride thro' Birchip[1] (I think they call the Vale) in spite of my vexation about the vile roads, which are truly quite unfit for a Gig to pass through & with any other driver than Tom I durst not attempt to enter one in this Country— Most happy should I be to travel as far as my feet could carry me, Yea most blessed! by thy side in this Country— but loth should I be to see thee either alone or with any one with thee, attempt to drive a Gig— Rain came on in the Even^g & Joanna & I who were the only *Ladies* that ventured, were obliged to stay all night & Tom fetched us home yesterday morning— and a sweet ride we had— for the sun shone & the air was much more mild & to day the weather is the same & I hope it is likely to continue fine—
I have, since I read thy dear letter been to walk with my aunt the rest are gone on business to Kington— here is a letter come from Jack to Tom— I wish its contents may be favorable to our wishes. — Little Totts is very happy— The Donaldsons are still here they are now riding on a swing which I think is good exercise for Tom— he & I often have nice talk about thee & I had sweet thoughts of thee in my dreams last night: dearest William how I do love thee! I hope I shall be no more anxious— in any other way than by those yearnings that I would not wish should be supressed, till we meet again— let me hear from thee often very often & tell me all. I must now leave off to dress myself for dinner the Kington party will be return-

[1] Burling Jobb.

ing— I wished to say a little to thee this morning, for I shall not have much time for a long letter tomorrow as we are going to dine at Nill— I could well excuse these parties on my account— but it cannot be— I have read the "Ladies calling" one of thy books— which pleased me much— it is such a book as Mrs Luff would say would do *her a deal of good*— I am going to begin with this single volume of Burnet History. I wish you may meet with the other. — —

We are to go to the Devil's Bridge & to the Wye— I should much like to have thee with us on these excursions— but I think I must not put aught off that is proposed on that account— because when you are here they may be busy, or the weather may be bad— besides, my having been there, need not prevent our going again if it can be managed, when thou canst be with us. which of all earthly things I should enjoy. — by the bye after I sent off my last, I remembered that I had forgotten to alter the word *Wye* which I had inadvertently written for Dee— if you noticed this you would think it was like thy *muddy headed* Mary. God bless thee—

Sunday Morn^g— Since I wrote yesterday & have had time to think about it, I have felt more thankful to thee than I can express, for your writing to me again so soon— for, calculating upon my having received your first letter I could not have found much fault if a second had not *yet* reached me & then how very miserable should I have been now— — I am indeed most grateful to thee for this kindness— bless thee continue to write whenever you can— I hope you will get plenty of franks & then you will not grudge sending me a few lines, when you have not leisure for a longer letter.— This is another sweet day— we shall have a pleasant ride to Nill but I regret having to be stewed up there over a fine dinner— We have all been weighed this morn^g. I weigh 7 stone 13— 3 pounds more than M.M. & 2 pounds more than Joanna— Tots only 2 s-12 lb this seems very very little, yet compared with Mary Donaldson who is 11 years old & is but 1 stone heavier it is not to complain of— —

John's letter to Tom is most dishonourable to him— I will not vex myself with repeating its contents to you, as you will have an opportunity of seeing it when you are here.— it is enough to say, that I do not think Tom can settle any thing with George, in justice to Henry, till he has had an interview with Henry— John is vexed that Tom does not think it worth while to go about signing the Papers relative to the Estate &c & the whole spirit & contents of his letter is most unworthy,—

I hope you will shortly get the unpleasant business of C.s[2] off your mind— what you tell me of him in connection with the Beaumonts is most shameful— I expect your next will tell me something about *Johnsy*— be sure to remember me to him & try to send us one of his little Books— I cannot get Tom to have any pleasure in his book— all he looks to is the end of his lesson— I take all possible pains with him to no purpose— I teach Mary & Jessy their lessons at the same time with him in hopes that this may settle him— they leave us on Wednesday & unless he gives his mind more to it after they are gone than he has done hitherto— I shall never think of leaving him behind me, should it be wished for— — There is nothing like a good School— You will have heard that [?dear] John[3] is not yet admitted to school on account of the *faver* that has been at the Parsonage. Dearest Love lose no time in calling upon Lord Lonsdale— for I am sure we ought to quit that place, & it would be a pity to remove at a time when we were subject to a second removal, so much of our time has been devoured I dread to look forward to a continuance of trouble of that sort. —

I am writing in the sunshine, the pool dancing before me— what would I not give to wander with thee in the opposite meadow that looks so green & so beautiful— the trees by the pool & the one in the court are ready to burst into leaf, but there is not a *green* leaf to be seen, except upon the goose berry trees & here & there upon a shy hawthorn that has been in compleat shelter— nothing here is more forward than at Grasmere The Gardens that we heard talked of at Kendal are far before any thing I have seen— the Cottagers are only now

[2]Coleridge.
[3]Johnny Wordsworth.

beginning to put the Spade into their little Plots. & our farmers are the only ones who have gotten all their seed into the ground— tomorrow they are going to send two Teams to help Mr. Urwick.

Monday Mo^rg^ I am going behind Mary with this letter to the Post— perhaps we may meet with your old one, so till you hear whether it is cast up or not, do not trouble yourself to repeat what you told me before. — What a most beautiful place Nillcourt is & what a nice Church yard— I never saw a Gentleman's dwelling so much to my mind— but I merely saw it from the road leading up to the Church— You & I will walk thither & wander about the whole of it— Joseph Stephens seems to be a most worthy Man, & they have two of the sweetest little Lasses I ever saw. — I have some hope of a letter from Grasmere to day— Oh my William dost thou not often think of those little Darlings at home— I have heard another instance of the good effects of Electricity, in a case of Paralasis— I hope they have received the Machine. Your dear little Willy will have become a fine talker before we see him again. —

The pool is like a Mirror this Morning— I trust you are well & able to enjoy this fine Weather. Dearest William I do love thee deeply & tenderly & most eagerly shall I look to the day of our meeting in the mean time take care of yourself & let me know all your doings— & any thing you hear of Public affairs that is interesting will be very acceptable here— I fear poor Miss Lamb is still in confinement— if not give my kind love to her & to your Brother Christopher when you meet with him— his Wife must be a strange one— You were very good to write to George so soon— God in heaven [ble]ss & preserve thee my best beloved— Make my respe[ctful] remembrances to Sir G. & Lady Beaumont & believe me [to] be thy faithful & affectionate M. W.

If Mr Curwen is in [To]wn perhaps you might do good to poor Geo by calling upon him— I suppose we shall be seeing Geo here soon as it is not likely that he can meet with a situation soon

Tell me when you have any account from Annette I am somewhat anxious for her next letter— I wish you had accompanied us to Oswestry Shall you send any Money to her, or wait till the Young Man calls upon you for some?— farewell

11

William to Mary, 2 May 1812

Friends who helped William to achieve a reconciliation with Coleridge praised his patience, tact, good sense, and integrity, but he must have been deeply grieved to learn that Coleridge had labeled him his "bitterest Calumniator" in a letter to Richard Sharp (24 April 1812). The £100 Wordsworth mentioned was the loan requested by Charles Luff; Thomas Woodruff, a colleague of Charles Lamb at the East India House, conducted other financial transactions for Luff. The melodramatic, controversial speeches of Sir Francis Burdett, the wealthy radical member of Parliament for Westminster, earned him a reputation as a seditious firebrand. Here Spencer Perceval, the prime minister, rebutted his attacks. Josiah Wedgwood was the son of the famous potter; in 1798 he and his younger brother Thomas had bestowed a lifetime annuity of £150 on Coleridge, but Josiah withdrew his portion in 1811.

Dr. Andrew Bell originated the "Madras" system of education, in which more advanced pupils instructed beginners. The Reverend William Johnson and William Wordsworth had used the method in the Grasmere school before Johnson left that post to work for Bell in London. Ann Dowling, a friend of Letitia Luff, was governess for Lord Galloway's children and later became mistress of a school at Ambleside attended by Dora Wordsworth. Henry Richard Vassall Fox, Baron Holland, played a prominent role in whig politics and wrote political history; with his wife he made Holland House a glittering center of Regency culture and fashion.

Earlier in 1812 Coleridge had completed a series of fifteen lectures on Shakespeare, Milton, and the principles of poetry. This second series was advertised as a course on Shakespeare, with background material on poetry, drama, and the stage. Coleridge's lecturing style was erratic—often brilliant, but occasionally tailing off into allusive obscurity. Although the size of his audiences diminished steadily, the lectures were highly respected. Captain Charles William Pasley was director of the Royal Engineers Establishment at Chatham; William had enthusiastically and copiously praised his *Essay on the Military Policy and Institutions of the British Empire* (1810). William Sotheby was a versifier of limited talent; time has confirmed the validity of Wordsworth's assessment. Sir James Mackintosh—reformer, statesman, historian, and philosopher—had recently returned from an appointment to an Indian judgeship; his "recantation" was a withdrawal of earlier criticisms of William's poetry. George Philips was a business partner of Richard Sharp. Samuel Rogers, poet and banker, was celebrated for his literary breakfasts. J. F. Tuffin was a friend of Rogers and the author William Godwin.

The comedy that William attended at the Lyceum on 30 April was Alicia Lefanu's *The Sons of Erin, or Modern Sentiment*; the tragedy at Covent Garden on 2 May was Arthur Murphy's *The Grecian Daughter*.

Saturday Morning before breakfast
I am looking for a Letter from thee my dearest Love; I hope thou hast duly received mine:— first let me speak of C's affair. Upon this I have seen Montagu & Charles Lamb. Montagu is very willing to be confronted with Coleridge, but he insists that this should be in the presence of some conscientious & serious person. I have therefore begged of Lamb to communicate my sentiments to Coleridge; & to tell him that I insist upon such meeting taking place; both on my own account & his; in order that nothing may be said by [him] of my conduct towards him but what has been established by all the concurring evidence which the case admits, and that if I am to suffer in his good opinion he may precisely know to what degree I[1] ought to suf-

---

[1]William wrote "to."

fer. Would you believe it. I have seen a Letter in which without naming me, though clearly meaning no other Person he calls me his bitterest Calumniator, describes the agony he has suffered in consequence of the behaviour of one (meaning me the same person) who had been in his heart of hearts; and states that his late journey to Keswick had convinced him that he had not been deluded— and accordingly being now certain of that he has recovered his tranquillity, and his very appearance is improved in consequence, &c— I was permitted to transcribe the passage which [will] be copied for you, by Dorothy; I would have given you myself the very words now, but I destroyed the slip of paper yesterday, after I had copied in a very short Letter which I wrote to Grasmere. This conduct is insufferable and I am determined to put an end to it. I am not at liberty to say to whom this letter was addressed, on account of some other business contained in it. I also know that he has spoken to the valued friends under whose roof I am in a manner which almost calls upon me to put an end to all intercourse with him for ever—

The trouble of hunting out Charles Lamb & settling the business with Montagu some engagements I have had beside, have prevented me from touching yet in many affairs but to day I purpose to take steps for having the 100 £ paid in to Woodriffs hands. On thursday night I was at the play, the Lycaeum, where I saw some good comic acting, and last night at the House of Commons, where I was a good deal entertained by a debate Upon the subject of Barracks. Sir Francis Burdett made a most intemperate and injudicious speech and was ably replied to by Perceval. Sir Francis however as far as words go speaks very elegantly & well. The Question was whether Barracks should be built at Liverpool, Bristol, and in Mary-Bone in London. This was objected to by the Opposition on the ground of Expense, and the extravagant plan on which it was proposed to raise these Buildings; and on these points the Opposition were so strong that they I think could of carried the question had it not been for the Indiscretion of Sir F.B., who drew off the attention of the House from the point of unnecessary expence, and opposing the proposition upon the ground that these barracks were part of a system to enslave the people by the means of the army, made use of such offensive expressions, and conducting his whole argument so like a factious demagogue, that several of those who meant to resist the erection of these Barracks, voted for them, very absurdly no doubt, lest by their opposition they should seem to participate or sanction the arguments & opinions of this ill-judging Sir Francis.

I breakfasted with Sharp on Thursday, he will supply me plenteously with Franks, and has kindly allowed me to have my Letters directed to him, which he will forward by the Penny Post. Therefore, Sweet Love, write often and long; and tell me every thing you do & feel. How I long to see you again! The Debate continued till near 12 Last night, and I was not in bed till One; but I contrived to rise this Morning before eight to write to thee my Darling; and I am happy to tell thee that upon the whole my health is much better; though yesterday I felt my Stomach much burthened & disordered by the indigestion which I felt in course of my conversation with Lamb upon the subject of Coleridge. — I do not know that I ever was more rouzed in my Life; and I feel the effects in my stomach at this moment. —

Sharp gave me the Order which admitted me into the Gallery of the House, and was so very kind as to come & sit near me twice or thrice for some time, to point out to me the different Members and give me every information which I required. He also during an uninteresting period of the Debate introduced me to the coffee room of the House where I had a comfortable and refreshing cup of Tea. A little before twelve, when the business was over, and I was waiting in the Lobby till Sharp came out, I noticed a person also waiting there whose face I was sure I had seen before, but who it was I could not make out. When Sharp appeared he accosted this Person & he turned out to be Josiah Wedgewood. He did not recollect me, but had noticed me & took me for a Member of the House; He says I am a much thinner Man than I was when he knew me. — Sharp's attentions were really most obliging, and I can tell you a circumstance in regard to Coleridge most highly to his Credit; so that with all his foibles he really has a world of merit. — Montagu wishes that Josiah Wedgewood should be chosen as Arbiter in the affair of C— & myself. —

I am happy to say that Miss Lamb is something better, and Charles seems to think the dawn of her recovery is at hand. I called on Tuffin in the City whither he is now driven in consequence of an endangerment of his property to the amount of twenty thousand pounds but 18,000[2] of it Sharp thinks he will recover. His Letter was very kind and expressed great regret that I was not under his roof. Montagu's present appartments are most sumptuous; and assuredly nothing would there have been wanting to my comfort. De Quincey is out of Town I guess at Oxford. Johnsy, I called upon the day before yesterday. I found him in a nasty Dirty place the temporary School. He seems quite pleased; but he finds Dr Bell in some respects a troublesome Man to deal with. — The confirmed change of circumstance &c had decayed Jonsy's health, and he described himself as having been extremely ill; but he has now gone through the seasoning— — I hope to have two or three pleasant interviews with him; but it is astonishing how little one's time turns to account in this huge City, especially when one lives as I now do at one extremity of it. Richard[3] is in the north. Observe I mention things just as they pop into my head. I have had a brief Letter from Luff, transmitted by Miss Dowling but she did not say when I am to call upon her. I shall call on Lord Holland, and indeed upon every Body. —

On Tuesday the 12th Instant Coleridge is to commence a course of six Lectures, One guinea the course upon the Drama. This is a most odious way of picking up money, and scattering about his own & his friend's thoughts. Lady B— has taken 30 tickets, which she will have to force upon her friends and where she cannot succeed must abide by the Loss; in this way the whole probably of the expense of the Rooms Advertisements &c will be covered, and the rest the Lecturer will put into his pocket.

Did I tell you that I have written to George? I will also see Mr Curwen if possible. — But success in these things must depend upon Chance. Taylor still continues to teaze Sir George; who calculates that with the Lawsuit which was to have been

[2]William wrote 18–000.
[3]Richard Wordsworth.

tried at Leicester, and all other losses he will suffer by this Man's folly and madness to the amount of 1,000 £ an enormous loss! — What is T. Monkhouse's address, if any occasion should lead me into the City, I should like to call upon him— I will try also to find out Captain Pasley who was in Town lately. — In short I will see every thing and person I can— And I hope that by rising early I shall find opportunity to write to Grasmere, and to thee my darling long Letters. —

I wish I could make this entertaining. But so much space will be taken up as merely saying where I can go & what I do that, I am afraid that I shall scarcely be able to give those details which would embellish the subject. You will smile at this wish; as if I had forgotten that every thing relating to me, however dull in itself, must be interesting to you. How I long my darling to see thy face again; and little Thomas I am happy that his good Friends are pleased with him. How rich should I be if I had nobody in the world to love but you two; but blessed be God I am most rich in other treasures; and when I think of Grasmere too my heart overflows with joy. —

This morning I must devote two hours to the reading of a tragedy to be offered for representation, the Author that indefatigable Scribbler in Verse, Sotheby— One act Sir George L.B.,[4] and I have sate in judgement on. Thus far it seems well enough contrived for the stage, but the diction is intolerable for poverty and bad taste. Sotheby has called on me, and I have an invitation from his Wife, but I have not found time to return his call yet. — He is a good and honest Creature but a provoking Poet— a mock Poet of whom this Age produces such swarms. Sir James Mackintosh is returned, and as he took the trouble of sending me his recantation from India, I shall not avoid him. Philips is in Town. now possessed by the death of his Father of a large fortune, he is coming into parliament; and no doubt, as he is rather a soft headed Man, Sharp will have with the party the credit of every vote that his friend George gives. —

I hope Darling that thou wilt have no more dreams about my

[4]Lady Beaumont.

Breakfast party given by Samuel Rogers in 1815, by Charles Mottram, undated. *Standing, left*: John Flaxman, Walter Scott, James Mackintosh, Lord Lansdowne, Sydney Smith; *standing, center*: Washington Irving; *seated, left to right*: Richard Brinsley Sheridan, Thomas Moore, William Wordsworth, Robert Southey, Samuel Taylor Coleridge, Rogers, Lord Byron, John Philip Kemble; *standing, right*: Francis Jeffrey, Thomas Stothard, Thomas Lawrence, J. M. W. Turner, and Thomas Campbell. Crown copyright. The Victoria and Albert Museum, London.

teeth dropping out; but that thy waking & sleeping thoughts of me will be of a more agreeable nature— I had many anxious fears about the Gig and was most happy to hear of your safe arrival; I know how careful Tom was, but I could not pacify my mind, as the conveyance is so dangerous, and as the Horse was new to the business— At 12 to day I call on Rogers with whom I was indeed to have breakfasted, and we are now going to the tragedy so that I may possibly not have an opportunity of

[*127*]

adding to this Letter; but be assured I shall write as often as I can, but not so often as if I had not to write to Grasmere likewise. — I cannot bring myself to write to thee a too naked Letter stripped of those tender expressions which are only for thy own eyes. I cannot do it, and oh how much have I to say that I am not able and how much that I am unwilling to trust to paper. Remember our being together at Liverpool on Wednesday that day week how sad did I feel that you[5] were so far from me. Adieu Adieu

[5]William wrote "I."

12

Mary to William, 6–7 May 1812

Mary inquired about William's plans to go to Bury St. Edmunds, the last stage of his travels in the south of England, in order to calculate the date of his arrival in Wales. Bury was the home of Catherine Clarkson after ill health compelled her to leave Eusemere, the Clarksons' home on Ullswater; Thomas Clarkson, her husband, was an eminent abolitionist. Longman was William's publisher, and in 1809 issued his tract *Concerning the Relations of Great Britain, Spain, and Portugal . . . as Affected by the Convention of Cintra* in pamphlet form; this is the work to which Mary referred. Lady Diana Howard Fleming and her daughter Ann Frederica were neighbors of the Wordsworths. Lady Ann had married her cousin Michael, who succeeded to the baronetcy after her father's death. She soon left him to return to Rydal Hall, Westmorland, where, sickly and dispirited, she resided with her mother. When the Wordsworths moved from the Grasmere Rectory to Rydal Mount in 1813, they became the Flemings' tenants.

Wed. May 6th

My dearest William

I closed my last after telling thee that Mary & I were going to ride to the post, without the least expectation of meeting with any other letter from you except the old one that I ought to have had before— judge then of my delight both to receive that, & another dear letter from London— I cannot my beloved express to thee how very happy thou makes me. indeed I am the blessedest of all Women— Oh it is good of thee to quit thy bed to write to me! & I am sure early rising will be of service to your health— I am most glad you have advanced so far in the business of Coleridge— I trust by this time it may be wholly off your mind— then you will have nothing but pleasure to think of—

You seem to think that time in London turns to little account & *I* think comparing your doings with mine that you have far the advantage of me— for with the little I have to do here I seem to have no time to read— being always ready to creep into bed at a very early hour— The Day is past I know not how— Tom's lessons (which to be sure are many) a Ride or a Walk— writing to you or to Grasmere— with a very little work & sauntering chat over the fire consumes the whole of it. Your letter was very interesting— & it was so nice that I could read a good part of it for the entertainment of the fire side, which in this newsless place was very acceptable. I am glad you were so well amused at the House of Commons & was pleased with the proper attention that Sharpe paid you— it is very well that you have made such a convenient arrangement for Franks— If I had known that the letter from Windsor was to be sent first to Grasmere it would have saved me much anxiety for I would not have expected it sooner, letters are so very long in coming between the two places. You give a very nice acc^t. of the continuation of your Journey, but I should have been more uneasy, even than I was, about you if I had not been assured in my own mind that you would not have taken the top of the Coach at that early hour from Chester— Tis well however that you were no worse for it. —

John Monkhouse is gone off with the little Donaldsons to Penfannan this morning, Totts will have a sad loss of his comrades for they have been very good to him— he will I think now get into the way of going more with the Men & the Lads about the farm, they are all very fond of him— but hitherto he has kept the steady companion of the Girls, who are two sweet Spirits as ever were born— it is melancholy to think how they are going to be lost— perhaps when you come you might be able to make some impression upon Mr D if you were to talk to him of the injustice he is going to do his family— I think it would be worth the trial at any rate— Yesterday a party went to Kington to shew my *Aunt the fashions* she was delighted with her expedition, & brought home a most gay Cap— & Tom brought me a present of a nice new Bonnet, so you see they are doing all they can to set me off against I see thee again— Joanna takes great pains to feed me— but I doubt she will not have the credit of me she deserves— but I am very well, and after I am so much used to ride on Horseback, as not to suffer afterwards by stiffness &[c] I am sure it will be very good for me. —

If you had looked at your Memorandums you would have found T. Monkhouses address— it is 21 Budge row— (near the Mansion House) he will be very glad to see you. I am sorry that you found poor Johnson so far from being comfortable— I doubt he will regret the comfort of Grasmere— When do you think you will go to Bury? — I hope you will continue to have all your visits paid &c to be ready to go to Coleorton as soon as it is convenient for Lady B. to receive you there— I hope you may be able to go with them— for indeed Darling I shall, long before the time comes, be eager for our meeting— Mind call soon at Longman's to secure the Pamphlets & settle the account. I am glad you called upon the Ladies Fleming— I dare say you may be some comfort to that poor Young Woman— I shall like to hear the account of your conversations— I am going to walk & shall finish my letter in the Evening— I have been writing to Grasmere God love thee— we have pleasant weather, but easterly winds & frosty nights. —

Thursday Mo^{rg}— Mary & I are going to the Post— Joanna & I drank Tea yesterday with old Mrs Stephens A very nice old Lady, she enquired after you— We are going to have rain again I think— Totts has been unhinged for the loss of his Companions— he is a little nervous fellow— I have lately observed in him a constant inclination to make water without the power— In the Mornings he always has a copious discharge— but afterwards— this Mor^g during the time I was dressing him he attempted twice saying he always felt as if he wanted & strained himself— I first noticed this habit in our walks— If it should continue I shall desire you to ask some advice about it. He sleeps with me & perspires much I have cast his flannel in the nights but as he still perspires I doubt whether he would not be better with the flannel than without it— while I have him with me he can take no harm however. He looks & is very well. We talk of thee & our darlings at Grasmere perpetually— Blessings be upon thee my best beloved— take care of thyself & continue to send me thy nice letters untill thou comes to me thyself— for evermore thy most affectionate Wife

M. Wordsworth

13

William to Mary, 7–9 May 1812

Dr. John Stoddart practiced law and wrote leaders for the *Times*. Taylor was probably John Taylor, journalist and poet, who in 1801 had admired the second edition of *Lyrical Ballads*. Henry Crabb Robinson, a barrister, is best remembered today for his splendid diaries, coffers in which he diligently hoarded the remarks and opinions of his more illustrious contemporaries. He mediated in William's negotiations with Coleridge and proved a loyal friend to the Wordsworth family for many years. Sir Humphry Davy wrote verse as a young man, but dedicated himself to a scientific career. He vaulted to the rank of leading British chemist of his day with his magisterial research in electrochemistry, but a book on agricultural chemistry and his invention of the safety lamp for coal miners attest that his interests were practical as well as theoretical. Davy had married a wealthy widow, Jane Kerr Apreece, just before William's arrival in London. Mrs. Maling was the daughter of the physician and poet Erasmus Darwin and aunt of Charles Darwin, the evolutionist.

Allston's painting of Cupid and Psyche, which William described so evocatively, has unfortunately disappeared. Coleridge asserted that the coloring of this work had not been surpassed since Titian.

Thursday afternoon, two [o]clock
I received thy dear Letter yesterday morning; I have just finished a Letter to Grasmere; and did not mean to sit down to

write to thee, till to morrow, but I have taken up the pen, partly from the pleasure of writing to thee & partly because I dine to day with Dr Stoddart at Doctor's commons, and, though I have several calls which I wish to make, yet I do not like to set out upon such business, and have to return here to dress; I shall therefore dress before I go out, and content myself with making two or three calls on my way eastward. — I am sorry to say also that I am partly a Prisoner by force of my old Enemy, who has plagued me cruelly since I came to town; from my having been so much heated in running about, and perhaps also from drinking some little wine; which I cannot find out does me any good, and therefore I think, in spite of thy advice of leaving it off altogether. I have suffered also from another cause which I need not mention. —

How happy my sweetest Darling am I [to] hear of thy excellent appetite; strength will be recovered rapidly I doubt not if this continues. — I entirely approve of thy resolution not to put off seeing things till I come; do not this on any account, for the reasons you mention. As to the mistake about the Wye & the Dee I am sorry I missed it, as it would have entertained me; but my Eyes were guilty of a lapse on their part for I read Dee— I should have smiled at the blunder and rallied thee in thought with a thousand Kisses to justify and repay my cruelty. — I love thee so deeply and tenderly and constantly, and with such perfect satisfaction delight & happiness to my soul, that I scarcely can bring my pen to write of any thing else. — How blest was I to hear of those sweet thoughts of me which had flowed along thy dreams; sleeping & waking my Love let me be with thee as thou art with me! — But I must tear myself from this. —

Coleridge has declined to meet Montagu, and I think upon sufficient reasons: they are so hostile to each other that nothing good could proceed from bringing them together. He proposes instead to send me a statement begun some time since to be transmitted to Sara;[1] but discontinued upon hearing that she had decided against him. — But no more upon this irksome

[1]Sara Hutchinson.

subject in two or 3 days it shall be brought to a close and you shall hear the whole. — I should have risen this morning at 7 to write to you, but I was in such pain from my old enemy, that I thought it better keep my horizontal & easy position in bed— This is a cruel hampering for me: I think I am worse to day on account of over fatigue yesterday. My Stomach upon the whole is stronger than it was; but I am dreadfully bound in my body. — I hope that less fatigue, and more care, will bring me ease. — I have seen Dr Bell, Alston. They both dined here on Wednesday. — Alston is slim & somewhat lank & delicate in appearance, seeming taller than he is with jet-black hair, and a complection out of which the colour appears to have been taken by a hot & relaxing climate. But his features though small are animated and intelligent. My old Friend Taylor was of the Party and Alston did not talk much, but seemed to enjoy greatly what was said. He was elegantly dressed, his clothes perfectly well made and well chosen, so that as I have told Sara she would have been quite satisfied with him in this respect. — —

Sat. Morning. Here I was interrupted. I should have sent you off a short Letter before— but I do not find it easy to procure Franks. — It seems to be looked on in London as a considerable favor. — I am surprized and rather alarmed that I hear nothing from Grasmere. — I have now two Letters from Coleridge unopened. The last which I found on my return yester evening, but that I had determined in consequence of a conversation with Dr Bell, and with Henry Robinson upon the subject (to both of whom Coleridge had previously introduced it), not to call upon C— for this Statement as if he asserts therein what I know he has asserted elsewhere, Montagu and he must give each other lie. I therefore gave to Henry Robinson a commission yesterday to wait on Coleridge which I think will bring the business to a close and in my next to be written I hope soon, you shall have the results. — I shall breakfast again with Dr Bell on Tuesday when I meet Johnsy. — I was much pleased with his good sense yesterday, and the knowledge of human Nature that he showed. I had also a long conversation

with H. Robinson, not a little interesting. He seemed to
apprehend that there was in Coleridge's mind a lurking literary
jealousy of me. I totally rejected that supposition, and told him
that I believe in my soul that envy & jealousy of that kind were
faults of which Coleridge was utterly free, and that if he had
not chimed in with my praises it was because he was in ill-
humour with me, and not because he was uneasy at any com-
parison between my intellectual Powers and his. Robinson is a
very clever man, and seemed sorry that he had dropped this
suggestion, as I should be most sorry to think that there were
any good grounds for believing it. —

I sate near an hour with Alston whom I found in his painting
Room; his pictures are all left in Italy except one, the Cupid &
Psyche. I will describe it to you. Imagine to yourself, for the
size of the Picture, the back of good large folio, in the centre of
this place standing rested two naked figures a male & femal[e]
human in every thing but their wings, their naked bodies front-
ing you but their faces inclined with an expression of enthusiastic love towards each; the figures are erect but rest against
each other; the flesh is beautiful painted white and almost
luminous & shaded off on the outline of the form; they stand
upon the edge of a bluish brook, that plainly reflects their
forms, and in the arbor of a dark green grove, whither they are
supposed to have retired after a shower, the ground being yet
moistened & freshened with the rain drops. Cupid, not represented as commonly like a boy, but a tall young Man has wings
tipped with purple like those of an angel, and Psyche as tall for
a female as he for a male, has short wings something like those
of a butterfly. The figures appear to be about a span long, and
are beautifully painted. I did not presume to give any *opinion* to
Alston upon this Picture, but I begged he would permit me to
mention the impression it made upon me.[2] The pleasure, I
said, which I have received would have been greater if my *surprize* had been less. I had much pleasure but it did not unite
smoothly or instinctively with my mind. — This effect I attribute to two causes, partly the style of colouring not resembling

[2]William wrote "it."

any Painter or school of Painters whose works I am acquainted with and which might in some degrees have *prepared* me for the sight of this picture, and still more from a cause which is possibly a defect in the picture itself, viz; the too strong contrast between the body of white in the two naked figures & the gloom of the groves behind them & in which they are standing. Could not I continued, this defect if defect it be, have been avoided by treating the subject differently; viz; by diffusing a luminousness from the two supernatural figures that should have died away gradually among the surrounding objects. He was struck with these observations, and said that he thought that a[3] better picture might have been constructed upon that plan; which he would attempt if he ever repainted the subject.— I think Alston both as a Man and a Painter is likely to answer the commendations bestowed upon him by Coleridge.—

Yesterday at a route I saw Davy & his new Bride; she is any thing but handsome— and full of affectation; never letting her features alone. Davy looks well. — Sir James Mackintosh was of the same party & his Lady— I have seen no new Man that has interested me but Alston, and no female except a Mrs Maling, a daughter of D[r] Darwin. She is only about 20, but a sweet & delightful woman, lively, with talents, and wholly without affectation. — I could not conceive how with such a father, she could become so engagingly simple and natural a Creature; but was told afterwards that the Doctor never interfered with the management of his daughters— a happy omission for them! This is the only woman I have met whom I could like you to see, in order that you might be pleased and know too what I admire.

Having an opportunity of getting this Letter franked I must close it this moment. Adieu you shall hear from me again I hope in three days at farthest— —

[3]William wrote "he."

14

William to Mary, 9–13 May 1812

William appears to have been correct in speculating that letters from Dorothy had gone astray; a tally in one of her surviving letters indicates that she sent more than he received. To economize the family addressed letters for William either to Charles Lamb*e* at the East India House or to Richard Sharp*e*, a member of Parliament, both of whom were exempt from postage payment. Lamb and Sharp forwarded the letters through the London two-penny post. (For his outgoing correspondence William regularly procured franks from members of Parliament.) The system saved the Wordsworths some postal fees, which were high, but cost them some letters—and anxiety.

George Canning, an influential Tory politician, had served as foreign secretary in the cabinet of the preceding administration. Spencer Perceval, the prime minister, was shot in the House of Commons on 11 May 1812. John Bellingham, his assassin, wildly sought revenge on the government for his bankruptcy; he was tried in the Old Bailey on 15 May and hanged on 18 May, after the court set aside his plea of insanity. For William the event symbolized the moral and political chaos of his time. The old king on the throne, George III, was insane. His son, the flamboyant prince regent (who became George IV on his father's death in 1820), was almost universally disliked or despised and seemed far more adept at self-indulgence and dissipation than in steering Britain through protracted war with France abroad or confronting economic crises at home. Again and again William reiterated, in the letters that follow, that the country was in a deplorable or alarming state. He was not exaggerating for rhetorical effect. The barbarities of the grisly Reign of Terror in France had not paled in his memory, and he feared the anarchy of a populace that appeared as hungry, angry, and desperate as the French had twenty years earlier.

Daniel Stuart owned and edited the *Courier,* the newspaper for which Coleridge wrote intermittently from 1809 to 1811. The chilling drama of the assassination and William's failure to see Coleridge all but obscure the fact that the two friends were reconciled. In a letter to Dorothy that William wrote upon finishing the one below, he hastily transcribed a copy of the statement he had sent to Coleridge, which finally healed the rupture between them:

I solemnly deny that I gave M— a commission to say any thing whatever from me to C—. All that I did say had reference merely to an apprehended Connection between himself and M— which I was convinced must prove injurious to both; nor did it ever enter my mind that by any possibility what of this pertained could any way affect the friendship and *intimacy* between [him] & me. Of course, and [?conclusively], and to meet C's statement in detail I solemnly deny that I commissioned M to say to C that I had no hopes of him. I also solemnly deny that I said C— was in *the habit of* running into debt at little Pot-houses for gin. I also affirm as sacredly that though in some of the particulars enumerated by C. as having wounded his feelings there is something of the *form* of truth there is *absolutely nothing of the Spirit* in any of them. As for instance, that I asserted that C— had been an absolute Nuisance in my family. It is little less than morally impossible that I should have used these Words, but it is absolutely impossible that either by these words, if used, or by [any] resembling them I could mean to express the impression of my mind and heart concerning C. or the feelings of my family in respect to him. So that in every sense in which the particulars enumerated by C and the whole of [?them ?originally] could, as evidences of unworthy behaviour on my part give pain to C, if he knew what I said under what circumstances I[1] spoke, with what Motive and in what spirit, I do give a most *solemn denial to the whole.* —

I have with the utmost severity of self examination looked into my own heart & soul upon this occasion and

---

[1]William wrote "is."

stand acquitted before my conscience of all blame except that I freely acknowledge an error of judgement in having suffered myself from any Motive however kind to the parties, & however pure to speak to a man upon so delicate [a] subject whose conduct is so little governed by the universally admitted laws of friendship and regulations of society in similar cases. #

Hoping to receive from C an assurance of his entire and absolute faith in this my disavowal I have to add that I fully believe in the truth of his Statement as an expression of his conviction that M— did say all he has ascribed to him. But whether the agitation in which C represents himself to have been from the first moment M— touched upon the business may not have occasioned him to mistake M— in some important points or whether M— may not have mistaken me; or how the misapprehension which actually [?subjoined] originated— these are points into which I do not deem it necessary to enter. The love and affection which I entertain for C— & which I trust he entertains for me do not require a solution of these difficulties.

If however C's mind still is troubled by doubts & misgivings as to the sincerity simplicity & integrity of the disavowal I have herein made I must then in satisfaction of my own honour require his consent to the first proposed interview between M— and ourselves; though aware that this would of necessity lead to an opening of the points in differences between himself & M which I think in itself very inadvisable.

Should this measure be rendered necessary by the state of C's feelings I beg that no farther steps may be taken till C— has closed the Lectures which he is on the point of commencing.— [DCP]

William Rough, a sergeant at law and poet, had been a close friend of William's brother Christopher at Cambridge. The Reverend William Lisle Bowles had earned a modest fame for his *Fourteen Sonnets* (1789). Lord Byron published the first two cantos of his *Childe Harold's Pilgrimage*—a dashing and sublime poetic travelogue—in March 1812, after which, he remarked, he awoke one morning and found himself famous; he was lionized in London drawing rooms that spring. In his satire *English Bards and Scotch Reviewers* (1809) Byron friskily swiped at Wordsworth, Coleridge, and many other contemporary poets and critics. *The Devil's Bridge,* an operatic drama, was written by Samuel James Arnold; *High Life Below Stairs,* by the Reverend James Townley. The lines of Milton that William quoted come from *Paradise Lost,* IV, 445–447.

Saturday night 10 oclock.

My dearest Love,

I have just returned from a walk of an hour and a half, for it has taken that time to go to and come from Baldwyns gardens, whither I went with the intention of sitting an hour with Johnsy, had I found him at home. My way back led me by the end of Newman street where the Montagu's live, and I had an hour & a half of the night to spare, but I preferred coming home, where I knew I should be alone, in order to write to thee, which is the most grateful of my occupations. To day I have sent off a hasty Letter to thee, abruptly closed; and have also received one with which I find no fault but that it is too short. But is it[1] not strange that I hear nothing from Grasmere? Surely a Letter must have miscarried; I wrote to them last Thursday. I hope all is well, but if I do not hear soon I shall begin to be alarmed. —

Do not put Thomas his flannel on again; I understand that every body who has worn a flannel in the night, perspires for some time after they leave it off, the same as when they wore it. That is the habit of perspiration continues: It is not however unlikely considering how weak Tom is that he may continue to perspire, during the greatest part of the summer; but I am

---

[1]William wrote "it is."

sure that he would be much worse if he wore flannel. — I will call on Thom Monkhouse about the beginning of the ensuing week, and also upon the Addison's. — I wish to hear again from Annette before I attempt to send her any money. — I am less tormented by my old enemy than when I wrote last, though not free from inconvenience, and my stomach is I think some thing stronger. How happy should I hear that thou hast grown a little fatter with this exercise and improvement of appetite. Oh could I but see thee again in this respect which thou wert when thou came down the Lane to meet at Gallow Hill on my return with D— from france. Never shall I forget thy rich & flourishing and genial mien & appearance. Nature had dressed thee out as if expressly that I might receive thee to my arms in the full blow of health and happiness. I remind thee of that time in order that thou mayst try to put thyself into the same train as produced those delightful and cheering effects. Then thou hadst only me & D— to think of, now thou hast Me to think of, little Thomas to behold, and all our dear ones at Grasmere to play before thy memory, with our sweet little William, and all his pretty looks and harmonious tones to entertain & soothe & support and nourish & cherish thee. Tell me thou my love that thou dost some credit to thy pasture. Thou sayst that thou art the blessedest of Women and surely I am the most blessed of Men. The life which is led by the fashionable world in this great city is miserable; there is neither dignity nor content nor love nor quiet to be found in it. If it was not [for] the pleasure I find under this roof, and that I am collecting something to think about; I should be unable to re-sist my inclination to set off to morrow, to walk with thee by the woody side of that quiet pool, near which thy days and nights are passed. O. my Mary, what a heavenly thing is pure & ever growing Love; such do I feel for thee, and D— and S— and all our dear family. — Write thou to me long and tenderly, thy next letter, may be under cover to Sharp, and the next after to Lambe, to whom I shall say that I have desired thee to direct for me. — His Sister, he writes me, is returned, but much weakened by her long & sharp illness.

Sunday Morning. Here I was interrupted last night by the arrival of the Beaumont's. I waked this morning before 7, and lay half an hour in bed thinking of thee and Grasmere; I then rose, washed myself from head to foot in cold water, shaved &c, and now, the above occupations having employed me near an hour I sit down to continue my Letter to thee. — I find, that the hours in London agree with me better than those we keep in the country. I rise as you see something earlier breakfast between 9 & ten, have a luncheon, as it may happen from 12 to 3, dine as may happen between 5 & half past six, take a cup of tea or Coffee after but never any supper, so that if I do not chance to overeat myself at breakfast, my stomach is never over-burthened. I am still very costive, but in other respects I am considerably better, and look I think better. —

I hear nothing of interest in politics, except that [it] is apprehended that these riots may still become more general. It was feared, by government that a kind of general rising would have taken place in the manufacturing districts upon the 4th Ins^t. but it has been prevented. I suppose by this time that the number of troops quartered in the discontented parts is very considerable. — — But I hear little of politics; and therefore cannot write any thing which would prove generally interesting in that way. — Henry Robinson, tells me with regret, that the number of Spaniards serving in Bonapartes armies in Spain is considerable; not he believes voluntarily but frightened & forced by the French to bear arms against their Country Men. — He gives a most favorable account of the state of North Germany, and does not doubt that if our troops had gone thither instead of that miserable expedition to Walcheren the whole Country would have appeared in open insurrection against the french. — I shall go to the House of Commons some other day to hear Canning, and some others. De Quincey is in town as I learn from Mrs M— —² I wonder he has not found me out. Mrs M— says that he took fire at some thing that you said to him about the possession of the house, and retired from their

²Montagu.

Spencer Perceval, by George Francis Joseph, 1812. The National Portrait Gallery,
London.

House in great Indignation. He is quite mad with pride. Mrs M— says he looks very ill. —

I shall now lay down the pen for breakfast, when I again take it up I hope to tell you that I have seen Coleridge; as I expect Robinson this morning. Ever tenderly yours. Kiss little Totts for me; I will try to find out Mr Curwen perhaps Sharp will be able to tell me. I saw Tuffin yesterday, he has a trifle for me for the Greens.

John Bellingham, assassin of Spencer Perceval; artist unknown. Printed in *The European Magazine*, 1812.

My dear Love, it is now 9 o clock Wednesday Morning; I have been in Berner's street to call on C— but he was gone down to the Courier Offc to assist Stuart in writing upon the late most dreadful event the Assassination of Mr Perceval in the Lobby of the House of Commons. He was shot dead there on Monday last about five in the afternoon, by a man named Bellingham, formerly a Merchant of Liverpool. —

The business between C— and me is settled by a Letter. He stated, which I will send to you some future day an account of what Montagu said, Part of which I denied utterly, that is the most material part, and the rest though I allowed it had something of the form, I utterly denied that it had any of the spirit of Truth. But you shall have the correspondence. I hope to see Coleridge to day; his lectures are put off, on account of this event which has struck all London as I hope it would the whole Island with horror; that is all except a few of the lowest rabble— for they I am shocked to say are rejoiced. Last night I was at the play with Miss Lamb & her Brother. To day I dine at Ruffs with Christopher.

I have already seen Christopher, who is, & looks well. I breakfasted with Dr Bell and Johnsy yesterday morning; Johnsy will have a good deal of vexation in his new situation, but I hope in the end it will answer. Dr Bell changes his mind, I fear, often, and has something of a plaguy manner, but he is a most excellent Creature— — I have heard nothing yet from Grasmere, and therefore am sure that some letters must have miscarried. I am very uneasy upon this subject. I shall write a brief note to day to them; I should much oftener but I only procure franks by chance, though Sharp made me so kind an offer, yet I do not like to abuse his kindness. Do you however address to him still. — Tell me if Thomas's difficulty in making water continues— and I shall speak to some medical person. I am considerably better myself in health, but when I have made a conquest of my old complaint some of those injurious accidents occur & throw me back. I am now doing well, but I fear a relapse from the same cause— I have undertaken a disagreeable employment for Dr Bell; viz to select and compose with Mr Johnson's assistance 20 pages of monosyllabic lessons for Children. —

Montagu tells me that the Policy left by Luff as a security for the £100 is not worth a straw for me. Of course I cannot think of advancing the money; I called yesterday on Woodriff— to carry him to Montagus that he might hear this opinion; he (Woodriff)[3] was not at home, and I waited in vain upwards of an hour for his arrival— I am now writing in the gesso rooms where I have breakfasted with Bowles the Poet who is just gone: he is a man of simple undisguised manners, but of mean appearance, and no strength in his conversation but it is impossible not to be pleased with his frank and ingenuous manner. This Letter will be franked by Lord Byron, a Man who is now the rage in London, in consequence of his Late Poem Childe Haroldes pilgrimage. He wrote a satire some time since in which Coleridge and I were abused, but these are little thought of; and the other day I met him here and indeed it was from his mouth that Rogers first heard, and in his presence told us, the murder of Perceval. —

I wish I could make my Letters more entertaining, but I have such a number of disconnected particulars in my mind, that it is impossible to treat any of them with grace or interest. Besides, I feel as if every word, my Darling was thrown away, unless it mention some intelligence of importance relating to Friends, or unless it be employed in giving vent to the feelings of my heart towards thee. oh my Joy & my comfort, my hope & my repose, what awful thoughts passed through my mind of thee & Dorothy and home soon after I heard, first or almost in the moment in which I heard, of Mr Perceval's death. I saw him only ten short days before his death upon the floor of the house of Commons, and admired the spirit and animation with which he suppressed & chastized that most dangerous & foolish Demogogue Sir Francis Burdett. It is most probable that the murderer on that very day was about the House of Commons, for he has been lurking there for more than a fortnight, watching an opportunity to perpetrate the execrable Deed. The debate which I heard on that day, must have had no inconsiderable influence upon the mind of this detestable fanatic; and the lower orders of the People in London cry out Burdett for ever in the Pot houses, deeming him their champion and the Man who is rid them of all their sufferings real

---

[3] William inserted the name between the lines; parentheses mine.

and imaginary. The country is no doubt in a most alarming situation; and if much firmness be not displayed by the government confusion & havoc & murder will break out & spread terribly. I am glad that I am in London at this crisis, I shall see and hear all I can; but I am melancholy in finding how one's time slips away in going after people whom one cannot find; besides this ugly affair of Coleridge which I hope may now be considered as settled, has hampered me grievously; & defrauded me of many days & hours of days. —

My sweet Love how I long to see thee; think of me, wish for me, pray for me, pronounce my name when thou art alone, and upon thy pillow; and dream of me happily & sweetly. — I am the blessedest of Men, the happiest of husbands— How often does that passage of Milton come to my mind; "I chiefly who enjoy so far the happier lot, enjoying thee, preeminent. &c— apologize for me to Mary Monkhouse & John for not having seen their Brother, but I have been really run off my Legs or a Prisoner in the House by appointments. On Sunday Morning Josiah Wedgewood called & sate above an hour with me; he has not had any communication with Coleridge for seven years, He spoke very kindly of him, and offered himself as a mediator, disagreeable as it was, the subject having been mentioned to him by Mrs— M—. I will not quarrel with Mrs M— but such has been her conduct in this case and others, and towards us all, that I must find some excuse for not placing myself under her roof. More of this when we meet. Tell me frankly can you puzzle out this wretched writing; if not do say so & I will write better; there is nothing which I would not do to give you pleasure, I would sit up all night, I would rise at midnight, nay any thing could I bring myself to without difficulty, which you would not condemn as injurious to me. My soul is all day long full of tenderness to you & my dear Grasmere friends. —

Miss Lamb looks far better than could be expected and enjoyed herself much at the play; a stupid opera, called "the Devils Bridge, but the Farce "High Life below Stairs was very entertaining; it is an excellent Piece. It is now half past 12 and at two I must be in Grosvenor Square to meet Johnsy, upon the subject of those monosyllabic books. at a quarter after three I must start for Ruffs, where I dine at four. I now proceed to write to Grasmere; how uneasy I am in never hearing from them, what can be the cause I sometimes fear a relapse of this frightful [?complaint]. I shall write again I hope on Saturday; and as often as ever I can. a thousand tender kisses, do write long & often Love to every body. Kiss Thomas. W W—

15

Mary to William, 13–14 May 1812

London news traveled capriciously to the provinces, but word of the Perceval assassination penetrated to Hindwell within forty-eight hours. The "Champion" was the former employer of Mary's brother George, when he worked as a bailiff and steward in Lincolnshire. George Sutton, who proposed to visit Grasmere, was a prosperous magistrate of Durham and uncle of Mrs. John Hutchinson; he adopted the Hutchinsons' eldest son, George, as his heir on the condition that the young man bear the name Sutton. Bessy Hutchinson was John Hutchinson's eldest daughter, by his first marriage. Basil Montagu's son Algernon lodged at the home of Mrs. Ross in Ambleside while attending the Reverend John Dawes's school there. Izaak Walton published *The Compleat Angler* in 1653; Mary reminded William to buy the book several times.

Wed. May 13th

I thank thee for thy very dear letter which I received on Monday— I felt inclined to write in answer the moment I had read it, but have restrained myself till this time— I wish my love thou couldst but tell me that thou wert quite free from that plaguy complaint, which hampers thee so much— If you think that a little wine really does you harm I would leave it off at once & not mind my advice— but I certainly did think that a little stimulant might be serviceable— tho' it is possible as you do not labour at this time it may heat you & make the Piles worse. You can try the effect of this change at any rate. You gave me a very lively image of the Picture indeed— & I think Aldstone must have thought your remark a most valuable one— I seem to feel the justice of it very strongly. I am glad you like Alstone & oh I do wish you had gotten to the end of your disagreeable business. —

After my heart had been refreshed by reading your letter on Monday, Mrs Donaldson Mary M. Tom & I set out each upon a horse to Eywood & a most glorious ride we had— a round of 10 Miles without the least fatigue or fear on my part, on the contrary I never enjoyed riding on Horseback more in my life— & in point of *cowardliness* it is the opinion of all here that I am less of a coward than She who had given me such a bad name. Sarah[1] has no great credit as a bold horsewoman here. I was quite glad to find that you had never been at Eywood— for I promise myself very great delight in accompanning thee to this Park— it is a beautiful ride round by Knill, & back thro' Kington— Knill Court is a most lovely place & seen to very great advantage on this road.— I enjoyed myself thoroughly, felt all the way how happy I should be to go over the same ground with thee & how much thou wouldst enjoy it with me— Only one thing that time has robbed me of had I to regret— & that is, the very great weakness of my eyes & this I feel most painfully when looking at the Country— they are indeed become very dim & I cannot see any thing at a distance without straining them very much, nor look steadily at any thing without an almost immediate painful indistinctness coming over every thing— they are grown much worse lately— I think this has been caused by their being so much excited in the course of my journey— encreased perhaps by the very little, & very little it has been God knows, that I have read since I came here— I must however begin to husband them well to preserve what remains to me— perhaps by care they may grow better— the appearance of them Tom says is much changed, he is sure that the squinty eye is very much more drawn in than it used to be

---

[1]Sara Hutchinson.

& M.M. is of the same opinion— I do not exactly see this myself— but I feel as if they both were smaller than they used
be. But enough of this— depend upon it I will take care of
them. —

George arrived here yesterday in very good health & Spirits.— He looks uncommonly big & gross— at first this made me
uneasy— but when we came to examine him we found this was
far more owing to the *unwieldy* manner of his dressing himself
& to the *make of his coat* than to his natural appearance— his
coat is far too little for Tom & in Tom's coat he looks quite a
different being— We can discover nothing in him to blame—
Tom says it is quite impossible that he could stay under such a
Man as the Champion— it is only to be wondered at that he
should have remained in his place so long— The whole country dispise him & of course G. must have had a hard task to
perform— doing the will of such a one. — G. sends his best
thanks for your kind letter, which he says laid 4 days before he
received it, so as he was about to set off here he thought he
need not trouble you with an answer— he had written to Mr
Curwen & if you could call & do any thing for him either with
him or any other Person G. would be greatly obliged to you— I
do wish poor fellow most earnestly that you could be the means
of getting him another place— Your being in London is a most
lucky thing for him— I do indeed think that you may recom-
mend him with confidence— Since I spoke to you before of
Jack— Tom has had another letter from him speaking of
George's having quitted his place, which he *says brings things to a
point*— & he requires Toms answer to the proposal he had
made about settling— the *proposal* was such as Tom had no
wish to settle till he had seen Henry— however in consequence
of this spur, Tom answered John's letter & wrote in the same
letter to H. telling him what he meant to give up to him &
George, provided John would do the same to G. & satisfy H.
or, as John seemed rather to wish that he *Tom* should take the
whole of George's part upon himself, that he was willing to do
so *immediately upon his hearing from H that he was satisfied with
John's intentions*— this, as I think John is now bound to shew it to
H., will bring things to a close. In John's letter he begs the

favour of you to enquire if Mr de Q would lett his Cottage[2] to Mr Sutton for a short time if he is in London or if you can write to him will you ask the question immediately & let me know the result— I do not think that the little Man durst do such a thing either for fear of his Books or his Housekeeper— What do you think of Dorothys taking the 2 Children, (when Sara[3] goes her Visit to Kendal), to the Sand side with one of the Servants, leaving the other at Home to take care of the Cows &c sending John[4] to Mrs Ross's and letting the Sutton's have our house or John might stay at home with Fanny or Sarah[5] & go to School— this would be most convenient for them, as they could be supplied with Milk Butter &c in the house— and they ought to pay more than would stand against the Sand-side party— would it not be a nice method, provided D— liked the plan, of getting a little fresh air for them all— When you write to G.[6] & write immediately, mention your opinion upon the subject & say to them about what time you think we shall be returning to Grasmere in order, if this plan when they have it proposed to them should be approved of, that D. may have some notion about *the time* that we could be able to spare the House— I shall write to them upon the subject immediately that they may make up their minds against we have Quincey's answer. I hope you have ere this got your mind at ease by a letter from Grasmere I have not heard lately, but I hope there is no cause for being anxious— they want me to take a ride so God bless thee for the present— We have glorious weather now— fine showers— the Landscape is most lovely at this moment. such a close, rich greenness!— —

Wed. afternoon. We had a ride about the fields— I upon Ginger Poney (Totts before his uncle & proud was he)[7]— which offers to carry me very well— so it is to be the steed that is to

[2]Dove Cottage, Grasmere.
[3]Sara Hutchinson.
[4]Johnny Wordsworth.
[5]Sarah Youdell.
[6]Grasmere.
[7]Mary wrote the words in parentheses between the lines; parentheses mine.

accompany the Gig when we take our travels— as soon as the foliage is a little forwarder, perhaps in a fortnight Tom Joanna & I are to go the Monmouth & Chepstow round— I most likely shall generally be the Horsewoman, as more confidence is placed in my performance in that line than in Joannas— The Devils Bridge Jaunt is to be, Tom says, deferred till you are with us, so you must take this into your calculation when you speak of the time of our return to Grasmere— I am now going to begin a letter to them & shall finish this tomorrow morning. Our darling little William was 2 years old yesterday.—

When you are any where near Sloane Street pray call upon Bessy Hutchinson & remember Mrs Addison's Bernards St you have both these addresses amongst your Memorandums [Tom Monk]house wishes much to see you & I should like you to call [on h]im, he is I am sure a good Creature— most exceedingly disinterested generous & charitable. Tom[8] caught 7 lbs of fine Trout the other day in the Pool— I wish you could buy the Complete Angler for me. I want to make Tom a present of it. I think you ought to bring a new fishing-rod with you for Tom complains of his being broken.—

Wed ev^{ng}— We have been thrown into the utmost consternation & know not what to think or what to do with myself, having heard that Mr Perceval has been shot in the House of Commons. — this is all we know but I fear it is too true— Tom heard of it from a Person who had read the dreadful news in the Hereford Paper— We have seen Monday's *Farmer's Journal* in which no such acc^t. appears— it must have happened on that day— I hope there will be some further news from thee tomorrow— if not a contradiction of this report— for this suspense is terrible— — I cannot understand this sad wickedness— What do the wretches expect? if it had been the Prince's life that had been taken their views would to me have been more intelligible— But surely the loss of this Man, tho we may not have such a one to put in his place, will not change the Measures he was supporting! — I wish you were here to give me something like

[8]Tom Hutchinson.

quiet— & to be out of the way of the distress & consternation that you are in the midst of— tell me all your feelings on this sad sad event. We have just now learned from the Postmaster at Radnor that this intelligence was sent from the Gen. Post Office on a slip of Paper, simply stating "that Mr. P. was shot on Mon. Afternoon at the door of the House & that the Assassin was immediately seized, that he was a Person who was formerly confined as a Lunatic"— Bad as this is, it is some satisfaction to think this act could only be done by a Lunatic— We were fearful that it was some dreadful Plot which might now be raging, the first act only being gone through— Alas for this Country, Who have we now— I fear a shadow pated Creature to take his Place— —

Thursday Geo & I have been at the Post— I had a faint hope of a letter from thee, tho' I did not much expect it— I long to know how you have stood this terrible shock. — I fear it will have made you very ill— We have rec^d. Tuesday's Star which contains a full account of the affair— surely the man is insane— — there may be a letter from thee tomorrow, we have now a daily post at Radnor— it is a pleasant ride thither. you will be glad that I enjoy riding on Horseback so much— You would be glad likewise to see what good spirits poor G. is in. I am sure from this he has conducted himself properly I do hope you may be able to serve him— God in heaven bless thee my dearest love— I feel daily more & more what thou art to me & wanting thee how poor all things would be to me—
My heart bleeds for Mr Perceval— O William that Murderer was perhaps with thee in the Members Gallery last week!! I would thou wert in my arms again— tell me all things & believe that my best thoughts are ever [with th]ee— Geo & Joanna will take this to Kingt[on] [   ] [d]inner I did not carry it to Radnor as [   ] I might wish to say something after I [   ] the Post— Joanna had a letter last Sat. [   ] they were all well thy faithful loving Wife M. W.

16

William to Mary, 16 May 1812

William began this letter on a blank space in a letter from Sara Hutchinson and Dorothy, which he was forwarding to Mary. He continued writing on a previously franked piece of paper but discovered that he had inadvertently selected a sheet addressed to Dorothy in Grasmere.

The "Monster" to whom William referred was the assassin John Bellingham. Gilbert Wakefield was a distinguished classicist and political idealist. His daughter Anne had married Charles Rochemont Aikin, a physicist and chemist, who was the nephew of the celebrated bluestocking and poet Anna Letitia Barbauld. William Roscoe, a Liverpool businessman, wrote verse and histories and collected art. The young man with whom William wrangled was probably Roscoe's eldest son, William Stanley Roscoe, a banker and poet. Recalling the disagreement in later years, William labeled him a "very shallow fellow."

Darling,
The accompanying which I received Yesterday, has relieved me from much anxiety I have a frank for Monday, for you and hope to write at some length on that day, therefore I have less regret in now saying so little— I have just finished a pretty long Letter to Grasmere. Lord Lonsdale will be in Town next week, and I shall make a point of seeing him; and then I shall

deem my *business* in London *done* and shall be most impatient to get away to thy arms, where alone I can be happy; unless when *Duty* calls me elsewhere. And I am sure that no obligation of duty will then exist to divide us. For as to amusement &c unless I felt that it contributed to my

contributed to my health &c, you shall know how the sentence went on but first let me tell you what a blunder I have made & this moment discovered, viz, that the rest intended for you has been written, by mistake on the cover, directed, *Miss* W— for Grasmere. A most unlucky oversight! for unfortunately there are some tender and overflowing expressions of Love which were meant for no eyes but thine, and which if I cannot erase, I must not send the Cover; for example I feel that every thing I had written[1] in the way of amusements appears worthless and insipid when I think of one sweet smile of thy face, that I absolutely pant to behold it again. Of course this must not go, and how to get rid of it I know not. — I have crossed and recrossed the Frank and part of it I fear will still be legible; at all events the very attempt to hide, will I fear give offense. — I have now blotted the sheet so that it is impossible to make out the obnoxious expressions— so let it pass; for I know not how (now that [it] is so late), to procure another frank, and I promised to write, against Monday. —

This morning Stuart called on me; he has been ill, is much reduced, and looks, I think, ten years older than when I saw him last. The complaint originated in a disorder of the Stomach which he ascribes to having often over eat himself, particularly when exhausted. He says that for some years he has had intimations that things were not going on well, in his constitution such as giddiness in his head, languor occasionally, and falling asleep after dinner. — — He had a discharge of blood & slime which brought him to the edge of the grave in a few days. — He is a most able Man. His good sense & knowledge of things are consummate. I wish that the ministers would take his advice for there is a sad want of knowledge & of firmness and

---

[1]William wrote "I had written every thing."

the Country is in a most awful state. The Monster is to be executed on Monday Morning I hope to procure, by means of the Poet Bowles a stand upon The top of Westminster Abbey whence I may see the Execution without risk or danger. It takes place on Monday Morning. I long to be with you for this London life does not agree with me because If I am ever thrown out I cannot find leisure to recover. —

Did I tell you that Mr Henry Robinson took me to Mrs Charles Aikens, Daughter of Gilbert Wakefield. She is a most natural & pleasing Character but there unluckily I met the whole Gang among the rest the old Snake Letitia Barbauld. I had an altercation with Roscoes son upon Francis Burdett, & was so disgusted with the whole Gang save the Hostess that I was made ill. I had further to run a couple of miles to prevent my being locked out here, as I gave a general order that they were not to be sat up for me after 12. — I think of consulting some Physician upon the costiveness I feel & the great quantity of thin mucous which is involuntarily discharged from my bowels. It certainly implies that the stomach & bowels are in a most disordered State. Tell me how you are mind if you gather flesh.

Adieu. Best love to every body; I will walk into the city soon or perhaps to see Monkhouse. I have been obliged to get a new suit of Clothes with a new hat & silk stockings

I cannot take leave of thee my beloved wife, on the other side of the Sheet. oh love me! & take care of thyself.

17

William to Mary, 17–18 May 1812

William alluded only passingly to the "state of the Country about Nottingham," but the discontent seething among the mill workers there genuinely dismayed and alarmed him. Insurrections had erupted in Nottingham the previous November, and in the ensuing riots, looms, newly invented stocking frames, and entire mills were destroyed. Violence fired the sheriff to call in the cavalry and infantry, but the disturbances spread. Workers complained of want of employment, the introduction of machinery to replace labor, and the high price of provisions—especially grain.

The French prisoner for whom William sought Daniel Stuart's help was Eustace Baudouin. James Montgomery wrote religious verses and hymns. John James Morgan, a lawyer and businessman, had been a friend of Coleridge for many years, and Coleridge made his home with the Morgans when Basil Montagu's indiscretion precluded his living with the Montagus. Antony Harrison, solicitor and poet, lived at Penrith in Cumberland. Edward Thurlow, a minor poet, edited Sidney's *Defense of Poesy*, prefaced by sonnets of his own composition, in 1810; the sonnets were reprinted in 1812, when his *Hermilda in Palestine* appeared.

Andrew Bell published his first booklet on the Madras system of education (based on pupil teaching) in 1797. It was slightly revised and reissued several times in the following ten years. The larger volume that William mentioned was published in 1808.

Sunday Morning half past 11.
My dearest Love,
It is a wet morning, at least it drizzles. Sir G. & Lady B. are gone to church, and I sit down to write a few words to thee on the cover of this frank which will go tomorrow. — Yesterday I dined alone with Lady B— and we met Lord Byrons new poem which is not destitute of merit; though ill-planned, and often unpleasing in the sentiments, and almost always perplexed in the construction. At half past nine I dressed for a party at Mrs Philips (the Philips of Manchester) there I found a number, nay a multitude of people, chiefly of the connections of the opposition. — It is not worth while to mention their names; I did not stay above three quarters of an hour; for I am quite tired of these things; If you happen to fall into conversation with a person at all interesting, on an interesting subject, it is impossible to prosecute it; for either some body comes in between; or inclination of variety prompts or an obligation of civility enjoins, an attention to some other individual, and the conversation is immediately broken off. I have already neglected several invitations of this kind, and shall in future attend to still fewer; so that I believe that I should soon slip into as deep a solitude in London as in Grasmere. Lamb tells me that his Sister is well and that you may address to him as many Letters as you like; therefore Let there be at least two to him for one to Sharp— And do, my sweet Love, write to me often while I am here, and as long Letters as ever thou canst, even if they contain nothing but repetitions of tenderness & love. —

Coleridge dines here to day with Alston & Wilkie; I purpose this morning to call upon the Addison's it is late but better than never— I hope to see thee much sooner than I thought of; for the Beaumonts are so alarmed by the state of the Country about Nottingham that I should not be surprized, if they do not go to Coleorton at all this summer; in which case I shall be able to join thee a full fortnight or three weeks sooner than[1] I be-

---

[1] William wrote "that."

fore could venture to flatter myself; add to this consideration that I draw little benefit either for body or mind, from what I see here, and therefore upon the whole I think it far most likely that I shall not be very long before I find my way into Wales. —

Do not omit any opportunity of seeing all you can before I come; it will be enough for me to walk with thee by the side of that pretty Pool and to fish with thee beside me, and to see thee under the roof at thy good Friends. — Stuart will learn for me what can be done in the cause of the French Prisoner, I have not yet settled Woodriffs business, but of course I shall not advance the money if the salary be of no value. Farewell, my darling, I am going to call on the Addison's. again adieu. — I am invited to Montagus this evening to meet Mr Montgomery the Poet but I do not think that I shall be able to go, as it is not likely, that the Party here will break up in time. again farewell.

Monday Morning. when I had gotten some way from this house yester afternoon I found that I had made a mistake, supposing that the Addisons lived in Berner street the same street Coleridge is in whereas I believe they live in Barnard street, in consequence of this mistake I did not accomplish my intended call but turned in upon Coleridge, and walked with him & Mr Morgan to call upon Alston; from whose house we returned to Morgan's where I eat a biscuit, and we thence took a walk in the Park. — Coleridge Alston and Wilkie dined here; and we had upon the whole a pleasant evening; Alstone I like much, & will tell you more of him when we meet. Wilkie is not particularly interesting in conversation. — Today Christop[r] & Coleridge dine here; and I hope Stuart; from whom we shall perhaps hear some interesting facts. —

The Assassin has not been executed in Palace Yard as was first proposed; had that been the place I should this morning have been a Spectator in safety, from the top of Westminster Abbey: but he suffered before Newgate; and I did not think myself justified, for the sake of curiosity in running any risk. — I should have been miserable if I had brought my life or limbs into any hazard upon such an occasion. — We have not yet

heard what passed at the Execution. The man is unquestion-
ably not of a sound mind; but it is not a madness of the nature
which ought to exempt him from public justice. — His case
seems in one point of view very much to resemble Antony Har-
risons. viz, that he had brooded so long upon a particular train
of ideas, as to have been crazed upon that subject. But he is
justly amenable to a criminal tribunal on this account; that he
did not withstand as his reason would have enabled him to do
the earlier impulses of these crazy and vindictive passions,
which have risen at last by indulgence on his part to such a
height that they appear in reference to this action to have over-
set his reason. In that he is clearly liable to the utmost severity
of criminal justice, by having wilfully suffered his passions to
dethrone his reason: for what is his case but an unexampled
excess of those vindictive feelings, of that revenge, or (as L^d
Bacon calls revenge) wild kind of Justice, which in the shape
of anger malignity pride cruelty and intense & cowardly self-
ishness, produces so much misery in the world. Would it not be
a horrible thing, that the extreme of a Man's guilt, should be
pleaded as a reason, why he should be exempted from punish-
ment; because, forsooth, his crime was so atrocious that no
Man in his senses could have committed it? All guilt is a deviation from reason. And had such an Assassin as this been acquitted upon the ground of insanity, the verdict would have held
out an encouragement to all wicked Men, to transcend the
known bounds of Wickedness, with a hope of finding security
from law in the very enormity of their crimes. — I perhaps
have said too much of this; but do read the trial carefully, and
you will find I think manifest marks of an insanity of that spe-
cies into which by little & little a Harrison was brought, though
from feelings quite the reverse of this Man's; viz a delicate
apprehension that he had here an instrument of doing wrong
to others. — I know that A. H. had resolved at one time to
shoot Robinson the Attorney of Ulverston; and certainly his
mind in respect to that Man was in a state of phrenzy. — Tell
me if you coincide with my view of this subject. —

And now my darling let me turn to thee, and to my longing

to be with thee. Last night, and this morning in particular[2] I had dream after dream concerning thee; from which I woke and slipped again immediately into the same course. — I do hope & trust that it will not be long before we meet: Coleridge begins his Lectures to morrow, which I shall not be sorry to hear. I do not think, they will bring him much profit. He has a world of bitter enemies, and is deplorably unpopular. — Besides people of rank are very shabby for the most part, and will never pay down their five shillings when they can avoid it. The Room will probably be crowded to morrow because subscribers may bring as many of their friends without pay as they like. The next day, will I fear present a great falling off: and I am pretty confident that by the fair gains of his lectures he will be a loser. Lady B. took 25 Tickets which she has disposed of & received the money.— But you cannot form a notion to what degree Coleridge is disliked or despised notwithstanding his great talents, his genius & vast attainments. He rises every day between 8 & 9 or earlier, this I think a great conquest. But his actions in other respects seem as little under his own power as at any period of his life. for example Lord Thurlow a young Man lately sent him a volume of Poems which he has published, superbly Bound. The Poems have great merit far beyond any thing usually published Coleridge never looked into the Book nor took any notice of this mark of attention. of course the Young Lord must be bitterly wounded in mind.

adieu most tenderly thy Husband & friend.

I will send thee another copy of Bells longer work.

[2]William wrote "particularly."

18

Mary to William, 18 May 1812

Anxiously, Mary brooded about William's safety during the Bellingham execution, but planning her excursion to Tintern Abbey with her brother Tom and sister Joanna may have served as a healthy antidote to her fears. Dallam Tower, in Beetham, near Kendal, was the seat of Daniel Wilson. The incident Mary referred to is not known. Johnny Wordsworth had attended school in Grasmere, but began instruction at the Reverend John Dawes's school in Ambleside within the next few weeks. He walked the three miles to Ambleside morning and evening, Dorothy proudly told her friends, carrying "a Tin Bottle over his shoulder and a Basket on his arm" (*MY*, II, 30).

Monday May 18th

My dearest William

I have to thank you for a most dear letter which I received on friday & for the envelope which brought me dearest Dorothy's letter to day— for which with you I am very thankful, for your uneasiness had made me uneasy also— I should not have been anxious had I not known that you had been disappointed of letters, because D. said that if *I* did not hear from them I might assure myself all was well— but a small matter gives one the alarm where one has so much to love & so much to fear. My best beloved! I was not easy to read of thy intention to be upon the top of Westminster Abbey during the execution & I shall have no peace in my own mind till I hear from thee after this business is over— Who knows what the frantic Mob may lead it to— I am afraid to think of it & I sincerely hope that thy letter of to day may not be written till all is over. — Your Wednesdays letter brought me most comfortable news of your health— this on Saturday is a falling off & it disheartens me. certainly I would take some Physicians advice— but mind then that you abide by it— & pray do not agitate yourself by too much talking, nor be vexed with silly People like young Roscoe— I trust you will now have nothing more to endure on C's acc^t. — have you seen him? I am just sending off a long letter to Grasmere enclosing £20 for Sarah[1]— I am sorry to find she is growing so thin— I do think my beloved! that I am becoming a little fatter— they tell me I look better every day— I certainly am very well— but I now begin, with something of anxiety, to count the weeks of my Absence from thee & our little Darlings— It does good to my Soul to find that thy desires are so completely in[2] sympathy with my own— and with what eagerness should I urge thy joining me here directly— *if I durst* I was going to say— but how would this agree with the plans before laid down—

You say that after you have seen L.L.[3] your business in London is done & then no obligation of Duty will exist to divide us— but my Love art not thou first to go to Bury & then to Coleorton before I am to see thy blessed face again? tell me how this is to be— If you have done in London I hope that you will make your visit at Bury as speedily as possible, in order that you may be ready to *accompany* the Beaumonts to Coleorton in this way the least time will be consumed & I do not see that your visit at Coleorton need be above a week or 10 days at farthest— *May be* you have some thoughts of coming here first— & for *us all* to return by C.orton— would this make much difference in the expence of our journey? — certainly it

[1] Sara Hutchinson.
[2] Mary wrote "is."
[3] Lord Lonsdale.

would be a great gain for us to have so much more of each other's society— but I dare not think of this— All I beg with much earnestness is that thou wilt take care of thyself— but compare thyself with those that are well in things wherever you can agree & not with those that are ill— Stuart poor fellow must have had a Dysentery & sorry am I to hear such a bad acc.ᵗ of him but you are nothing like Stuart either in habit or constitution so do not dwell upon his weakness & your own— but think of all cheerful & loving things & keep your body open & I am sure you will be better— —

Tom is going to take my Aunt to Hereford next Friday & Saturday with Mary & perhaps George— Then if the Weather permits he accompanies Joanna & Me to Tintern Abbey, Ross, Chepstow Ragland Castle & I know not where— but I fear we shall be hampered with the Gig & often not be able to see things to the best advantage— But dear Tom is very good in wishing to shew me all he can— What would I not give were you but to be with us— O William it does seem strange that desires like these cannot be complied with— may not even be thought of— for circumstanced as we are I should *not like to think* of it with hope— had we but had that place that Dalham Towers robbed us of it might have been— I long to hear the result of your visit to Ld L.— do not be afraid to push him on the point in Question— —

Does not dearest Dorothy give us a nice account of our two little Darlings⁴— and dear John— by the bye I do think from all that D. has said on this [?subject] that John ought to go to M.ʳ Daw[es What] do y[ou th]ink? — I was sorry you had determined [   ] consequence of Montagu's opinion not to advance the £100 for Luff— I do think L. ought not to have made the request, but having made it, & you having suffered him to depart under the idea that he should have the Money from you— it seems to me that you are in honour bound to advance the sum required— & run the risk of the consequence— — If he lives there is no fear that he will suffer you to lose the Money & were he to die I think you would be sorry that you

---

⁴Catharine and Willy Wordsworth.

had refused it to him. I know well that you will make a far greater sacrifice to *duty* by refusing, than the loss of the Money would be to you— but I do not know that it is good for the heart at all times to be strict to the dictates of duty— I think you should let him have the money. Surely you will be hearing from Annette soon— —

I have written this in very great haste— wishing to send a few lines by this Even^{g}s post lest you should have thought me long in writing— do not be angry for the shortness of it— for my thoughts of thee are long, and deep & everlasting Tom is better— and his perspirations are less violent so I think what you say about the Flannel is just— he often talks of you, but of little William more than of any Body or any thing— he is doatingly fond of him— he is gone to the Plough this afternoon he wanted much to go to Kington fair this Morn^g. — Remember me with great affection to Miss Lamb & her Brother God bless thee & believe me to be eternally yours M. W

X X

19

Mary to William, 20 May 1812

Again the unreliability of the Wordsworths' makeshift postal mechanism distressed Mary, obliging her to repeat information she had conveyed in an earlier letter. Mr. J. Wheelwright was the business partner of Mary's cousin Thomas Monkhouse.

Wed. May 20th

My dearest William

I have just read thy letter finished on *Monday* and as there is no mention made of a letter which you ought to have rec^d. through Mr Sharpe on *Saturday* I am apprehensive that those sent to him do not always reach you— particularly as I find upon reading over Dorothy's letter which you sent in your last, that a *former* letter from her *also* meant *for us both* was enclosed to Sharpe, which letter you must never have received, as you would have been spared the uneasiness you had last week in consequence of D^s supposed silence. I have an opportunity now to forward a letter to Kington— so I write in order that you may enquire into this if the said letters have not yet reached you. I am rather anxious about my letter as I wished you immediately to make application to Quincey whether or not he would lett his House for a short time to Mr Sutton— I wish for a speedy answer because I am desirous for an *occasion* to write to John[1] in order that I may speak of George to him, as I know he feels unpleasantly towards him— G. not having written to John upon his quitting his Place— I have it in my power to justify George, & to write in most favorable terms of him— indeed I do feel that G. deserves to be thought well of & I trust you may be able to serve him. I am sure he must be a great loss to the Champion G. is so much interested in every thing concerning him &c, that it is plain— he has had the Champion's interest much at heart— I wish he could have staid but that was impossible & retain the respect that was due to himself— but you will hear all when you arrive. He would have had a wood sale about this time—

My heart dances to think that we shall meet sooner than I had hoped would be the case— next Tuesday if the Weather suits (& this day promises admirably) we set out as I told you yesterday to the Wye— we shall be absent probably a Week— in that time I can have none of these sweet letters from thee— but I will write: if I can, & O how I shall think of thee & *feel* for thee— when I am tracing this blessed river— —

In about a fortnight from this time the Wheelwright's who are now in Westmoreland &— are expected here— then we shall have a house-full & I should think & pray, that very soon after their departure, your Visit to Bury being paid, you will be ready to come to us. — I wish you may be able to serve Annette's friend[2]— I told you what I thought about Luff's business yesterday. — I think precisely with you about the Assassin— I have always said that his mind was not right but— that it was a sort of Madness or insanity that ought to stand in the way of his being punished never once entered into my thoughts— I am glad you did not see the execution. We have got no *full* account of his Trial— Friday's *Public* Ledger left off in the middle of his defence & we have not rec^d. the succeeding ones & the *Farmers Journal* only contains an abstract of the Trial Mondays Ledger is come so I fear we shall not see the concluding part of the Trial at length unless you could send it to us.

[1]John Hutchinson.
[2]Eustace Baudouin.

God in heaven love thee they [?are] sat down to Dinner & the
Man is waiting so I must break off— Bless thee again & again—
My yesterday letter was sent to Lamb— God love them both—
thine most fervently M.W.

   See Bessy H if you can— trust you are better

20

William to Mary, 23 May 1812

William opened his letter rather petulantly, disgruntled that the post had failed to bring him more letters from Mary. Later the arrival of a delayed letter and his sheepish discovery of a very substantial letter, tucked for safekeeping amidst his linen, assuaged his sense of neglect. In his *Tintern Abbey*, which he recalled again, William described how "mid the din / Of towns and cities" his spirit turned to the river Wye, in memory seeking and finding restoration, quiet pleasure, and a blessed serenity. His letter reflects this process, for, weary and ill from city mores and manners, he drew a healing tranquillity from imagining Mary in the peaceful landscape of the Wye valley. William transcribed his impressions of London as a much younger man in *The Prelude*. Then it had seemed a fair, a grotesque raree-show, a dizzying surreal spectacle. Most of the public figures William sketched for Mary in 1812 seem puppets from the same carnival.

Richard Colley Wellesley, Marquis Wellesley, had been governor general of India and in Perceval's administration foreign secretary; the older brother of Wellington, he was a statesman of considerable influence, though he never achieved the power he believed he merited. The crisis William referred to was the resignation of the cabinet ministers in response to a vote of no confidence from the House of Commons on 21 May. Because of personal animosities and political factions, repeated attempts to form a new administration failed, and on 8 June the prince regent requested that Lord Liverpool (Perceval's successor as prime minister) and his cabinet resume their governance.

William's unflattering portrait of Lady Davy betrayed a disappointment in Davy's choice of a wife shared by many of his friends. Dorothea Jordan, the celebrated actress to whom Wordsworth compared Lady Davy, was especially admired for her comic roles; she is thought to have written the farce *The Spoiled Child*, in which she played Little Pickle, a schoolboy. The work was performed in London during Wordsworth's sojourn. From 1791 to 1811 Mrs. Jordan had been mistress to the Duke of Clarence (later William IV). Henry Phipps, Baron Mulgrave, to whose dinner table Wordsworth sacrificed a fishing trip, held the post of master general of the ordnance in the Perceval and Liverpool administrations.

Mary Morgan was the wife of Coleridge's friend John James Morgan. Charlotte Brent was her sister. Concerning Coleridge, William referred Mary to a letter from Dorothy that he had just forwarded, which does not appear to have survived. His direction "See Dorothy's letter" concludes a page. He continued writing on a new folded folio sheet but found that he had written too much to include with the frank he had procured. He cut the sheet in two and enclosed the first part with this letter, dated 23 May. "This sheet last part of the Letter," his parenthetical note instructed Mary. The second part, beginning with the words "Boy among the number . . . ," he saved and sent with his letter of 30 May. The text is printed below as he wrote it, rather than divided as Mary received it.

Joanna Baillie, popular dramatist and poet, had recently published her third series of Plays on the Passions. The *Edinburgh Review* panned the work, attacking her literary principles as well as the plays themselves. John Wilson's *Isle of Palms* was published in February 1812.

Samuel Boddington and his business partners, Richard Sharp and George Philips, were West India Merchants.

May 23[d]

My dearest Mary

I am most unlucky in regard to Letters. Yester day I received from thee through Lamb a short one, in which mention is made of one sent off the day before and which I ought to have received through the same hand, but Lamb has never had it. I called on him yesterday after I had received the other & he tells me that no such Letter has reached him. By whom did you send it to the Office. I am heartily concerned at this; for your last is mortifying for its shortness. Indeed the whole of the Letters which I have received from you amounting to 4, dated April 23^d, another May 6th, May 13th, and the last May 20th, would not together make one *Long* Letter. I do not mention this by way of reproach but tender the language of regret to express my sense of the value of your Letters to Me. How unfortunate this last should have been lost, or delayed, I fear lost forever. And there can be no doubt but that a long one from Dorothy to Sharp is irrecoverably gone. The one from D— which I sent to day arrived yester day and you will read it with much pleasure.

As to Quincey I know not where he is; I have called twice at his lodgings, the last time a few days ago and was told by the Mistress of the House that he left Town five weeks ago with an assurance that he should return in a week: so of course I cannot consult him about his House. I have written to D— my sentiments about letting ours to the Sutton's, leaving it to her own choice. But I do not my self wish it; Catharine seems to be so well that change does not appear to be necessary; and one would not like to be kept out of our House, if we should either wish or be obliged by sickness or any other cause to return to it. — In fact I do not at all like [the] thing, as far as I am concerned, but as I said before they may do as they think proper. Depend upon it my dearest Love I shall make all possible haste to get to you, which I certainly shall be able to accomplish sooner if the Beaumonts do not go to Coleorton. — Chris^r is so much engaged that I am not likely to see any thing of him here, and he goes down to Bocking next week, to return when he takes his final departure I know not; but if it does not happen to suit with my plans I shall make no delay on his account, but will simply take a peep at Bocking, that is at Priscilla & her Children on my way to Mrs Clarksons. I am afraid she will be for detaining me at least a week; but if I stay any time at Bocking I can not afford so much. —

This Letter will probably reach you on Monday morning,

and on Tuesday you set off on your Tour; I hope not on horseback, I am sure it would fatigue you & do your health no good— fatigue is sadly injurious to invalids and to those who are not strong. Do find time to write to me, you cannot think how dear your Letters are how precious they are to me.

Surely by taking a little pocket book You may have a Letter going forward and may finish it by snatches, at those intervals when you are resting. I was half hurt when you said that you would *"write if you can"*. Can there be a doubt that you may. — I was not hurt at this if, as indicating a languor of affection on your part, I know you love me as much & as deeply as it is possible for woman to love man, or Wife to hold dear her husband; but it seems to me an indication and almost a proof that you were not aware of the delight & happiness with which the sight of a Letter from you filled my heart. — O Sylvan Wye thou Wanderer through the Woods how often has my Spirit turned to thee! — I shall now have a thousand added reasons to think of this Stream with tenderness when I know that you are pacing its banks. —

As you cannot receive my Letters I shall not write again till towards the close of the next week; in the meanwhile let me tell you that in respect to my old enemy I am much better; but my costiveness still continues; and I am feverish & turn & perspire a good deal in the night. In fact this style of living does not upon the whole agree with me; I mean when I dine out, as the dinners are so very late never till 7 or after, and being asked to drink wine, I don't like to refuse. But above all too much talking fatigues me, something I suffer too from hurrying about the Streets. — Will you be interested in hearing that the new Ministers have given in their resignation, so that of course Lord Wellesley and Canning will come in I hope without any of the opposition. The Country is in a deplorably distracted state; and for my own part I have no confidence in any public man or set of men; I mean I have no confidence in their Knowledge & Talents; and as to integrity the Marquis of W— is a desperate profligate, and Canning is a man whose character does not stand very high— Coleridge gives another Lecture to day; I hope it will be more popular than the last which was much complained of for its obscurity.

Sir Humphry Davy, by Thomas Phillips, undated. The National Portrait Gallery, London.

I have breakfasted twice with Sir Humphrey & Lady Davy; she is a good natured woman with considerable cleverness but her Manners are bad, she never lets her features alone, & gesticulates & dances and bends like Mrs Jordan acting the Spoilt child. All this has originated in affectation, but she now does without knowing what she is doing, it has become natural to her. She is a plain woman, thin & tallish, very dark complexion, and a wretchedly bad skin [?not] tawny but black, that is the blackest I ever [?saw] on any english Woman. She rouges her cheeks very high; but assuredly uses no white paint for her neck and breast. She would wear out my [   ] her unquiet manners; but I think Davy may [   ] [hap]py with her, fond as she is of admiration, [   ] has an infinite fund of Kindness & good nature. On Monday I was to have gone with them in their Barouche upon a fishing Excursion to some little stream about 10 miles from London, but most unluckily I found myself engaged to dine at Lord Mulgraves an engagement of full three weeks standing. I am truly sorry for this; as I am sure that I should have enjoyed the day much and it would greatly have refreshed me. Davy will let me have a rod & some tackle to bring to Hindwell, he says he will lend it me I hope he will give it; in about two months or less they are to be at Lanterdine¹ (do I spell right?) I mean the place on the Teem near Knighton, and if I am not gone into the North we are to have a meeting. Davy appears to have attained wonderful skill in Angling; and I should like him to try his strength in Hindwell pool, but he says that the finest fishing is in the preserved Brooks near London, that there [are] many spots of this kind where he can pull as many Trout as he likes from 3 to 5 pounds weight, and that in some they make a point of throwing back into the stream every fish under two pounds & a half. His wife must either be very rich or very extravagant; for they live in an elegant house, in Berkeley square in the first style of fashion; but too much I fear on this subject. There is one disadvantage in this twofold duty of writing letters to you & Grasmere that I write so much which scarcely appears worth the

¹Leintwardine.

trouble of expressing twice, and still less do my Letters seem worthy of being sent from one place to the other, even where no expressions of tenderness have slipped from me that are unfit for any eyes but those for which they were intended.—

Yester day evening I drank tea with Mrs Morgan Miss Brent & C—[2] he seemed in good health & spirits,— but his face looks far too broad & full for complete health, though in other respects

See Dorothy's letter

(this sheet last part of the Letter)

I sate the other day at Sothebys. I like Miss Bailey much, her manners are those of an excellent English Gentlewoman; totally free from all affectation, & with a frankness that is most engaging & becoming. — I mentioned to her the late Edinborough Review in which I understood her last Publication had been most uncandidly dealt with, she said, that she could not deny but she was some what mortified, yet nothing like so much so as if the case had been less in the extreme. What I should have liked best, said she, would have been a favorable Review but as I could not have that, they have given me the next best thing, one in which they deny me all merit. Now the middle course would have hurt me most, and therefore I have some reason to be thankful. Mr Wilson is reviewed, & Miss B— who by the bye is no Witch in Poetry spoke highly of an Extract from the Poem which we had in Mss, to the sleeping Child and which is but an Attenuation of my ode to the Highland Girl. — I took no notice of this obligation, but simply said that some time since I had seen those verses in Mss, and thought that they were not without merit, but that as a whole they were very languid and diffuse. I learn from H— Robinson, that Mr Wilson is represented as my Scholar, but one who has surpassed his Master. I am sorry for this; and that it is so expressed or insinuated I have no doubt, as Lamb told me the same, I am sorry for it on W—s account as it cannot but be painful to him

[2]Coleridge.

& most probably will some day or other draw upon him a severe retribution from some of my Admirers, of whom I have more than you or I are aware of; and those who are so are devoted to me enthusiastically.—

My love, and dearest darling, am not I good in writing to thee such frequent & long Letters, Let me praise myself, — here has the morning Newspaper been lying an hour and a half beside me untouched, containing as I have heard most interesting Letters from Lord Wellesley & other great personages upon their conduct at this most interesting crisis. Yesterdays Newspaper also, containing the account of the debate, upon the Motion the result of which act was the resignation of ministers I have not read, having been engaged in writing to Grasmere. — —

Before I had finished this last sentence I was called down stairs to a conference with Sir George & Mr Wade his Attorney, & have had from him a Comment upon a Letter which Taylor has written to Sir George. Taylor's conduct has been most infamous and desperate— What is to become of him & his family I know not.— I will tell you more of this when we meet— — I am glad to hear so good an account of George; I have not yet seen Curwen, & scarcely know where I shall find him, nor do I hear of any person who is in want of an Agent, though I have made several Inquiries. — I will find Curwen if I can, Sharp would be the most likely perhaps to know his address, & him I expected to meet day before yesterday at Boddington's but was disappointed. —

Let me tell you an Incident.— As I was walking in South Audley Street I came to a Woman who with a small bundle of Papers in her hand was crying out— Here is the life of Bellingham who &c— There was a small group of people about her, and a little[3] Boy among the number, who seemed to doubt if the ballad-like Papers she was offering for sale, were really the Thing they purported to be. Yes says the Woman emphatically

[3]The note printed at the conclusion of this letter appears at this point in the manuscript, at the foot of a page.

pointing to their title which was in Large Letters, "life, and life he had, for his heart stirred about six hours after his Body was dead. This the Surgeons have declared, and you may read in the Newspaper of this *day*, and, so going off triumphantly she exclaimed, and a good deed he did." Nothing can be more deplorably ferocious & savage than the lowest orders in London, and I am sorry to say that tens of thousands of the Middle class & even respectable Shop-keepers rejoice in this detestable murther, and approve of it. People talk of the national character being changed; in fact it has been changing for these thirty or 40⁴ years during the growth of the manufacturing & trading system the Malady has been forming its self, and the eruption has now begun, but where it will end heaven knows— Depend upon it I shall keep out of the way of riots, I love you my dear wife & my Grasmere friends far too well to trust myself in the way of them. —

I received a few days ago a very kind Letter from Captain Pasley now I believe Major, in which he expresses his regret at not being able to see me in London; and expresses also his thanks for my interesting Letter; which he says, he often reads, and upon which more frequently still he meditates. He would have replied to it long ago, and took up the pen, but was unable to do justice to his ideas. This gave me great satisfaction. He is at present superintending a Military Establishment at Chatham for the purpose of qualifying Officers, and also a body of common men, to conduct sieges; In which department of service our Army is yet considerably inferior to the French but he hopes to make it as much superior. He invites me down to Chatham, and if I can go I will, and return upon the 2nd.

Both my time & paper admonish me that I must lay down the pen; the Carriage in a few Minutes will be at the Door to take us to C—s Lecture. Adieu my darling Love— I shall see T. Monkhouse & Bessy Hutchinson; the distance is so great or I should have seen M— long since. Love me & think of me & kiss little Thomas for me, and no account fail to write to me while upon your Tour, Best Love to every body— how ardently

---

⁴William wrote "4."

do I long to be with you. I half hoped that your missing Letter would have found its way to me this morning— but alas it is now 1/2 past two & no sight of it. farewell & take Care thy most loving Husband   W. W.

N. B. I have been obliged to cut off the other half sheet finding the Letter above weight

21

Mary to William, 23–25 May 1812

Mary began this letter on the same day that William wrote the preceding one, and it opens with the same woeful complaint. Love letters never fly fast enough or frequently enough. Nicholas Vansittart was appointed chancellor of the exchequer on 20 May 1812. The *Courier* that day printed a letter threatening the life of the prince regent if Bellingham was executed. Richard Addison and Richard Wordsworth managed the Wordsworths' accounts. Captain John Wordsworth, an older cousin of William, had retired in 1801, resigning his command of the *Earl of Abergavenny*, an East India merchantman, to William's brother John. The ship went down off Weymouth on 5 February 1805 and young John perished with her. Dora Wordsworth attended a boarding school for girls at Appleby, near Penrith, which was run by Sarah Weir, a family friend of the Hutchinsons. The village school at Grasmere was considered too rough for the education of a young lady.

Saturday May 23^d

My dearest Love,

Your *overkindness* in having written to me almost every day has spoiled me, & taught me to be somewhat unreasonable—for I am almost ashamed to say, that I felt disappointed when I saw at the Post office this morning, that there was *no* letter from thee— On Thursday I rec^d. the 2^d. Book you have sent enclosed in a blank cover— which *was* a sort of blank to me—

The first page of Mary's letter to William, 23–25 May 1812 (Letter 21). The Dove Cottage Trust, Grasmere.

at the same time I felt it a sort of earnest that you were in possession of another frank which was soon to convey to me some further communication of thyself— some of the same tender heart-breathings thou hast lately blessed me with— of course I was yesterday somewhat damped when the Newspaper arrived unaccompanied by a letter— & this mor^g. Joanna & I walked to Radnor, I in the full hope of hearing from thee— a delightful walk we had thither— but I could not help feeling sad on my return— & have all day since felt an unusual weight & sadness about me that I cannot shake off, without a little communion with my best beloved— I have therefore shut myself in my own room for half an hour to give vent to my feelings in hopes that I shall be better company below when I have done— at the same time knowing that what I write when my heart is thus oppressed will be, however stupid, acceptable to thine. I *do* long most intensely for the time when you are to join me here— I never felt this more than when we were walking through those greenest of all green fields this morning— the birds were singing, and the air was so balmy, & I seemed to have so much leisure (a thing which I seldom have at our own sweet home) to know how blessed above all blessed creatures I should be were you but here to wander with me, & enjoy the joys of this heavenly season— dearest William! the time will soon be here I trust, & long shall it be ere we part again— if this depends upon my choice— —

Yet I *do* not regret that this separation has been, for it is worth no small sacrifice to be thus assured, that instead of weakening, our union has strengthened— a hundred fold strengthened those yearnings towards each other which I used so strongly to feel at Gallow Hill— & in which you sympathized with me at that time— that these feelings are mutual now, I have the fullest proof, from thy letters & from their power & the power of absence over my whole frame— Oh William I can not tell thee how I love thee, & thou must not desire it— but feel it, O feel it in the fullness of thy soul & *believe* that I am the happiest of Wives & of Mothers & of all Women the most blessed— and, if it be gratitude to acknowledge this, not by words, but by actions— by supposing that this *must* be understood because it is so— that the spirit feels & it *must* communicate then William, I am the most grateful— not only to thee but to every thing that breathes & to the Great God the giver of all good— But I must stop or I know not whither I shall be carried & instead of composing myself by retiring I shall unfit myself for receiving the Party from Hereford whom we are expecting—

Tom drove my aunt thither yesterday,— & MM & Geo accompanied her on horseback— the weather has favored them much, & I think my Aunt will return much pleased with her Jaunt. — I forgot to tell you that there was a note enclosed to T. Monkhouse in that letter which ought to have been in London Last Saturday & which you make no mention of in the letter that you closed at Lambs at 3 oClock on Monday— nor has Tom answered the note— so I fear that the letter, which was sent to Sharp has not reached you— I have sent 2 short letters by Lamb*e* since that time which *I hope* you have received & that I shall hear of them & you tomorrow—

I wish you could but see how busy little Totts is riding backwards & forwards all day with the dung cart— this will do him good— he is too fond of housestaying when little Henry is not at liberty to play with him— he has a cold & he does not look well & I have sad work to keep him in subjection— I think the manners of the Women & Maid servants in this country have a bad effect upon him— he is with them nothing but "Mr *Thomas* & the *little Gentleman* & it is "would you *chuse* to do this— & please to"— and so on— that my Gentleman is like to forget himself in the Parlour & it is no easy matter to manage him— I often wish he was at School— but he is a sweet Boy & I think this journey will have made impressions upon him which will be lasting, & he will be better for it hereafter—

We got Wednesdays Courier today & find the new appointments in it— Do you hope any thing from Mr Vansittart? I know nothing of him— The threat to the Prince Regent is too much in the stile of a Black guard I think to be much noticed— but the state of the Country is certainly most alarming— The Provincial Papers are filled with nothing but accounts of riots— I cannot but think it unwise to publish all these things— Surely the prospect of such a plentiful year will tend to allay the *fears* at least of a continued scarcity— at present I fear it is too true that there is much distress amongst the Poor— We hear plenty of it in this house, for Tom is overseer of the Poor & we have the needy almost constantly at the door.—

Sunday   The business between John & Tom seems now to be settled— Tom has rec^d. a letter from John in which he says that he shewed Henry T's last letter & delivered to him the part addressed to him self in which T. states his intentions, as I believe I before told you, to which J. says, H. seemed inclined to return no answer being perfectly satisfied with Johns intentions towards him— which consist of a *promise* (which H. in case of John's life or death he has no doubt sets as much value upon as all the bonds in the world) of £40 a year together with house rent free, Coals Milk & Butter &c Of course this letter of John's is a perfect release to Tom from Henry & in every sense I should think a security— as H. chuses to be satisfied no one has any thing further to say about it & Tom is left at liberty to act in his own way towards George & I doubt not but he will settle with him immediately— John's letter would have pleased me better if he had not still harped upon his own claims in contradistinction to Tom's upon my Uncles property, stating that his doings should not be exactly measured by Tom more particularly as *he* John had already been a sufferer by George— now you Know this is a concern that ought not to have been thought of in the consideration of rectifying my Uncles will— & again he notices as another reason for his not doing any thing for George— *"Sirrah's Behavior towards him"*— (but this do not mention it would only make more ill blood between them) & again his large family! & concludes his letter with a hint that he would not have dwelt upon these things if he had not been provoked to it & adds that Tom would [n]ot have done it had he not been put upon it! — I a[m] rejoiced however that the business is at an end even in this way— — Henry's income will be quite sufficient as I suppose he has £40 a year or thereabouts of his own.

Rich^d. Addison arrived here this mor^g, he has been upon business in Glostershire — I wish he could have given me some account of having seen you, but he did not even *know* that you were in London. — The post has brought me no letter to day— Geo has just returned from Radnor— surely there will be one tomorrow as I told you that we should set off on our Journey on Tuesday & it would be a sad thing for me to go without hearing from thee— as it will be at least 6 or 7 days before we return & I now do not think that we shall get away so soon as Tuesday the Gig Harness requiring repair. If I have an opportunity I shall forward this today, else, I may possibly keep it to send by Mr Addison— By the bye I wish you would speak to him about having a statement of our money affairs— I would do this myself, but I think the subject will come more properly from you— I am sure we shall never be any nearer by applying to your Brother. You must be sure to bring plenty of money with you to take us home— — I long to know what hope of success you have from your visit to Lord L.[1] tell me all about it.

Monday Morning   I find Mr A. does not leave us before Wednesday, so I must send off my letter by this days post— I dare not enclose more to Sharpe till I hear that my former one has reached you— surely I shall have a letter to day. This is thoroughly a Summer's day, quite hot, but the beauty of this place is cruelly impaired by the quantity of weed that has spread itself over the pool— it has a nasty patchy look & a very unpleasant smell at times. Remember to bring I. Walton's book & I think you ought to bring also a fishing rod as Tom's is a broken one. Mr A. tells me that Capt. & Mrs Wordsworth are in London—

I have had no intelligence from Grasmere since the letter which you sent to me & I begin, not to be uneasy about them, but uneasy with myself that I do not hear again— it is a fortnight since that letter was written which seems a long time not to know what has past at home— Those 2 littlest Darlings how my heart does beat when I think about them! Dear dear William— dost thou not love them & that Darling little Dorothy at

[1]Lonsdale.

Appleby & dear John O how glad we shall be when we all get together again— Tell me if I do wrong by directing so often to Lambe— When do you go to Bury? Blessings on thee my dearest Love my thoughts are ever with thee & ardently do I long & continually do I think of the time when we are to meet— I have sweet thoughts of thee that I would not part with for all the Treasures of this life— adieu— I am going I believe to ride with Mr Addison

evermore thine M.W.

22

Mary to William, 26–27 May 1812

Poised for departure on her excursion to Tintern, Mary was grounded by the bungling of the local blacksmith. That delay proved fortunate, however, as the toothache whose arrival she recorded in her postscript worsened in the following twenty-four hours. Mary accepted the broken gig and her swollen lip doughtily, rueful only that the period during which she could not receive letters from William had been extended by half a week.

Tuesday May 26th

My dearest Love

Your letter with dearest Dorothy's enclosed, reached me yesterday & indeed it delights me to find that thou valuest my letters so much at the same time I am sorry, that you are dissatisfied with them— when you say that all you have rec^d. would not make *one long letter* I am sure more must have been lost than the one ascertained to be so— for I have written a great number— but I cannot say how many— The one in question, was the first I sent to Lambe he ought to have had it on Wednesday— it was given to a Gentleman of Radnor on Whit. Monday— together with a very long one containing a bill for £20 to Sarah— as yours has miscarried I am fearful about this— the Gentlemen are gone to enquire about them & I shall tell you the result before I close this letter, which I mean to send by R^d. Addison who sets off to Ludlow in the Mo^{rg}. the letter I hope will reach you on Friday & if you wish for further particulars you may call upon him— he & I had a delightful ride yesterday together with my Brother Tom to Eywood— I was mounted upon John M's Mare & was well pleased with my steed— it is to be the one we take out upon the Tour, as George's poney cannot carry a Side Saddle without laming the back— Do not my Darling be uneasy, or fearful that I shall be tired with too much riding— as Joanna & I shall take the Gig by turns. For my own part I would rather we could go *without* the Gig as it will be a sad hampering to our pleasure— & deprive us of seeing by the Banks of the Wye most that is worth seeing— I had hopes that we might have been able to have *sent* the Gig round by the road & have ourselves sailed down the River but this cannot be— for R^d. Addison saw a party set off in this manner from Ross the other day, & a Boat could not be had for less than £4.10 to Chepstow or £2.5 to Monmouth— so this plan must not be thought of— assure yourself I will lose nothing that any exertion without fatigue on my part can gain. But I know if you had been with us *I* at least should have seen more than we shall do— Tom says we must take what we can & be thankful You shall no doubt hear from me on My journey— but Joanna prays me to tell you that you are not to expect a fat Wife to come back to if I *worret* myself by writing so much— at any rate she says such work would keep her lean— By the by I do think with her that the pleasure of rec^g such letters as yours, & the writing, & thoughts of having to write in answer, is a sort of excitement that very much stands in the way of ones *feeding*— it is too active an enjoyment— but who would pay such a price for fat? Not I.

Sarah[1] has written to Joanna a delightful account of our dear John which I will send you if she can spare the letter. We are very much interested by your political snatches— I skim all the papers, but I have not the patience to wade thro', & try to understand all the ins & outs of the "interesting correspondence" as you call it between Ld Wellesley &c. — We have got no acc^t. of

[1]Sara Hutchinson.

the New Ministers in our Public Ledger— the Rascal of an Editor Now talks of hopes of New Men & Measures, hitherto he has been firm to the Ministry now he is proving himself to be a time-server & I shall have no faith in what [he] says in future— Your account of the Davys entertained me— thou dost like a bit of scandal connected with her Ladyship dearly— We shall be very glad to see Sir Humphry at Hindwell if he can be separated from his Wife, but we could not relish the thought of having to entertain a Lady of her stamp. I was much grieved to be interrupted at the beginning of the Incident which you were obliged to keep back.[2]—

I see that Dorothy is exactly of my opinion with respect to the state of Stuarts health— but perhaps what I said to you upon that subject was written in the lost letter— I need not repeat it however. But I do lament that you feel yourself so much deranged deeply— pray lose no time about having advice & take care not to harrass yourself so much— when you have done in London go to Bury & as I hope the Coleorton Journey is over make what haste you can to me, not to neglect Christopher or to leave Mrs C.[3] dissatisfied— but I do not really join with D. in pressing you to make a long stay with her— a week at any rate I hope will be the utmost that is necessary— M[r]. A[4] says your Brother Richard is expected in Town shortly. M.M. desires me to tell you that if you can get any letter Paper that is much cheaper than 2/ a quire, the price they are obliged to pay here they will thank you to bring them some— of course they do not like a shabby article. Be sure you buy something nice to take to our dear John before you leave London— They have a fine house full you see at Grasmere— I quite dropped all thoughts of the See-side scheme being adopted when I heard of the chance of your being here soon— M.M. keeps very well & enjoys the thought of accompaning us to Grasmere much. they are all overjoyed that you are coming— & Totts not the

---

[2]That is, the final sheet of Letter 20, which Wordsworth posted with Letter 24.
[3]Catherine Clarkson.
[4]Richard Addison.

least— what do you think of his (when we were talking of you this Morning in bed) clasping me in his arms & exclaiming "O my love & my life— O my sweet Mother"! he is a coaxing Monkey— — Mrs Urwicks children are here today playing with him & he is quite in glee. I fear there will be much difficulty in a situation being found out for George— if so they must be obliged to look out for a farm— I cannot think this will answer so well as an Agency of some sort But poor George has no time to lose & if he has not some prospect before him he will be becoming low spirited— at present he is in great heart. I fear Mr Curwen is not in Town— a few weeks back I saw that he was making shallow speeches at the Guild at Carlisle— but he may have left the Country since that time. I wonder we should have heard so much about your not calling upon the Ladies Fleming, I thought you had done great things by making them such an early Visit— perhaps you had made an engagement to go again which had escaped your memory. Always give my best love to the Lambs I am sad at what you say concerning them—

dear William I must now bid thee adieu. My hands are so cold I can scarcely drive my pen— I have been writing all the Mor^g first to Jack— then to Grasmere & now this letter which I could not but send by Mr A. tho' it is scarcely worth it— but it will shew you that I am willing to do my best— but pray do not measure my love by my letters— but o thou art more than good to write me such sweet ones I think we shall set off to morrow that is if the Weather keep fine— a shower is passing over at this time we intend to reach Ross tomorrow night I believe— Where next I know not only Friday is the day upon which we are to see Piersfield[5]— the place only being to be seen upon that day & on Mondays. — I shall not close my letter to night & of course if we do not get off in the morning shall add to it   God bless thee evermore   M. W.

The letters were duly put into the office at Radnor— I begin to fear for our journey— the Glass falls— I sent a letter to

[5] Piercefield.

Lambe since the one you have rec^d. dated the 20th I *think* bearing date 23 Wed Morn^g. Another disappointment! We were to have gone as far as Hereford this morning along with Mr A. but when almost ready to set off it was discovered that the Blacksmith instead of mending, had broken the Gig worse than before— we cannot therefore set off till Sunday as we must be at Piersfield on Tuesday as we cannot be there on Friday not being able to start early this morning— I hope this delay will be attended with one great advantage as it has determined us to take a 3^d. horse instead of the Gig, that is if we can have Mrs Urwick's easy Poney, which will be a much better plan than we were going upon— for I found in talking our journey over last night that we should see with the Gig comparatively very little as we were all the way to keep to the turnpike road & this after Tom's being at so much expence would have grieved me much— another reason that I do not lament this delay, is that having had the tooth ache (my front tooth) last night my upper lip is so much swoln this morning that perhaps by much exposure it might have been made very bad— You would think me an odd looking creature if you saw my mouth in this state— besides we do not think the weather quite settled, yet this is a beautiful Mor^g. *After all* I am very sorry that having purposed going, we do not go as I can hear nothing from thee for such a very very long time— As it is not likely you can receive this letter in time to write before Saturday there is no possibility of a letter meeting us at Hereford on Sunday Noon— so I will not desire you to send one for I hate the idea of running the risk of losing our letters.

23

Mary to William, 29–31 May 1812

In later years Mary appended a poignant memorandum to the end of this letter. Her grief shadows our reading of the letters that follow; for, though she received William's letters joyfully and wrote her replies in the fervent anticipation of their reunion, her brief annotations insistently evoke a different image of Mary as she reread these letters—numbed, and wondering how she could have been happy when she was never to see her child again.

Mary maintained her vigilance in searching out a post for her brother George. Here she suggested another candidate as an employer, the author Walter Savage Landor, who had recently purchased Llanthony Abbey, in Monmouthshire. Thomas Frankland Lewis of Harpton Court, near Hindwell, was Tom Hutchinson's landlord. The new deeds of title from the estate of old Henry Hutchinson were not yet signed; Mr. Clarke was the executorial solicitor.

On 31 May, recovered from her toothache, Mary set out with Tom and Joanna Hutchinson on their tour of the lower Wye valley.

Hindwell May 29th Friday

My dearest William

You are now exulting in this delicious weather for my sake, & enjoying in imagination, the thoughts of my being at this moment a Traveller on the banks of the Wye— tho' perhaps by this time you may have heard from my letter which I sent by Mr Addison, of our being disappointed in our intention to set off on Wed. Mor^g.— The weather since that time has been most favourable for such an excursion. When we rose this Mor^g. it[1] was raining very fast & had done so all night (after one of the most beautiful evenings ever felt or beheld) & seemed likely to continue raining— but it cleared up & is now most delightful— Yet notwithstanding all this we have reason to rejoice that we were prevented setting off, for, as I told you my face was a good deal swoln on Wed: mor^g., it was not bad enough to have made me give up the journey if all things else had favoured it— and it grew worse very fast & soon I was quite frightful to look at— indeed I was the exact pattren of D. at Coleorton when she had her new Tooth put in— the swelling is now very much fallen, though I have not yet got quite my own looks back again. — If we had gone I should certainly have blamed the journey for making me so bad as I have been, but indeed I believe we should have been obliged to have returned— Before Sunday I shall be quite well & I trust the Weather will continue to be favourable— I shall not forward this sheet before Sunday, therefore if I am not again disappointed I shall add a line to it at Hereford. I lament most exceedingly having spoken so confidently of our being away this week, for the want of your letters for so long a time is a sad blank to me. I wish much to know if you have fixed when you go to Bury & it will be an age before I hear, & am vexed at myself that I did not beg of you to send a letter to Hereford at *any rate* because I find we are to return that way. therefore if it had not met me there on Sunday it would not have been lost— as it is the chance of Sunday being past it is not worth while writing thither as we shall feel ourselves just at home when we get back to Hereford. Of course I have been quite a Prisoner for the last three days—

I was interrupted here— but this morning (Saturday) my face is nearly well, before night I hope it will be quite so— the

[1]Mary wrote "is."

rain seems to be gone & as the Glass is rising all things are going to be favourable to our setting out tomorrow— We have had no letter yet from Sara acknowledging the Money sent by the same days Post by which my letter that had not reached you was sent— I am very uneasy about this, for an answer according to my calculation might have been here last Thursday. — Tom is now upon the pool, he is a very patient fisherman & *sometimes* a successful one but he says they are tired he thinks of biting— perhaps the fish have been frightened we have had so many fishers lately— George *thrashes* (as Mr Addison says) the Water at a famous rate & I believe he never has once had a bite— Mr A too tried without success & Mr Lewis's Gamekeeper is very often here— I tell them you will teach them all how to *catch*, when you come, so mind you are well prepared for the attack—

Oh Darling I do wish you were here— it is seven weeks tomorrow since we left home & six this day since I parted from thee— You would like well to see little Totts skipping as he is this moment over a little feeder that runs out of a drain into the pool just in front of my window— he is very good in never going near the water without leave, or when he is wa[t]ching the fishermen— he looks very proud of his activity just now, but I think he will be getting a wetting— he is very much delighted to see them wash & shear the sheep & he tells me that he is to clip a Lamb at the Clipping— I hope he is now making some progress at his book— we are reading Lessons with two syllables & it is nothing but want of attention that prevents his learning very rapidly— I cannot get him to learn his lesson or his spellings by himself before I hear him— he will not look on his book— & this makes teaching him a long & most irksome business to me— & I have been fighting ever since we came against the practice of spelling every little word *to himself,* when reading to me, before he utters it, without being able to get the better of him— He spells columns of words of 2 Syllables wonderfully considering he has never looked at them before he comes up to spell— Yet after all, it is lamentable to think how backward he is compared to what we were at his age & what the Southeys now are— he is very well & quite happy—

I desired you once before, but as this request may have been made in the lost letter, I repeat that I very much wish you could buy for me the Compleat Angler— I want to give it to Tom, whom I think it would please very much. — What can that little maffling Quince be about? it is odd that he should not have contrived to see you in London— did you hear any thing of him from Dr Stoddart? — I wrote yesterday to Miss Weir that we might hear something of dear little Dorothy— we have had so little communication that way, that it almost seems as if the Darling did not belong to us— As affairs stand at Stockton I think Sarah can have very little satisfaction in going to see Henry, so if that Journey is to be given up, We shall meet little Doddles[2] at home on our return— I rather think Miss Weir will spend her Holidays here.

It is now Saturday afternoon between 5 & 6 oClock M.M. George & I have had a delightful Ride since Dinner— after 3 days confinement & a fall of rain what a delicious thing it is to get abroad again! My thoughts have been full of thee & of the pleasure which I hope we are to enjoy here together— o William I do long for the time— very little stiffness remains in my face & I feel quite fit to begin my journey in the Morning— We all go on horseback & you need not have the slightest apprehension of fatigue— for the exercise does not the least fatigue me— I am sure it is very salutary to me besides, we shall not take long journeys— I suppose we shall only go to Hereford tomorrow night— if we had had the Gig to change with each other if we *had* been tired, we might have gone farther— but I do not think that as far as pleasure goes this would have been any advantage— as dear Tom does not grudge the expence it is much more profitable not to hurry over the ground. —

Perhaps when you are at Bury you might be able to hear of some situation for George, if you continue unsuccessful in London— Tom says that if we hear of nothing likely to suit him before you come, that he dares say he can by application to Mr

[2]Dora Wordsworth.

Landor get one of his farms for him & in that case he should like you to go with them thither for it is a nice place that you would be pleased to see & he thinks it might be an advantage to them to have you with them— But for my part I should be much better satisfied if an Agency could be met with. I continue to be perfectly satisfied with George & Tom is the same. Jacks suspicions have all originated in the cause I named at Chester. Tom has to meet Mr Clarke at Shrewsbury early next month to sign the writings & I have desired John to send us an extract from my Uncle's will relating to our Estate in order that Joanna may have her will made before I leave Hindwell. —

Now my best beloved! I think I shall not again take up the Pen at Hindwell till about next week at this time, therefore from this room, which is become very dear to me from the sweet feelings which have here been excited in me— by thy letters— & from the many dear thoughts, hopes & expectations that have passed through my mind upon my pillow by the side of thy little Darling, let me on this side of the Paper bid thee a tender adieu— That thy best thoughts will go with me I am well assured— & that every object which I see that gives me pleasure will be ten thousand times more dear to me for thy sake thou wilt not doubt Dearest Love I am as happy as Woman can be wanting what constitutes that happiness— yet even *wanting this* I cannot but think that in the *thoughts* of my possessions I am the most blessed of all Women

Thy own Wife & Friend   M.W.

Hereford Sunday Night 1/2 past 8 oClock— Here we are in³ excellent spirits having had a comfortable Cup of Tea by a warm fire side— we set out after an early dinner & a showery Mo^rg— the weather flattered us all the way to Kington— afterwards we had rain all the way, more or less, hither— however our great Coats protected us well & we had upon the whole a very pleasant Ride— With a beating heart did I greet the Wye— O Sylvan Wye thou Wanderer thro the Woods!— — O what a verdant bed does it rest in where we first came in sight

---

³Mary wrote "if."

of it! I was most exceedingly delighted with this Ride— I dare say this Country, indeed it must be so, looks far more beautiful than when the season is[4] further advanced— when the leaves are in[5] full perfection— here must be too much wood— now it is perfection— The Chesnuts in full Blossom the Thorn the Laburnum & the Lilac— besides abundance of flowers in the Cottage Garden— The orchards shew little Blossom— the Peartrees & cherrys are over & there is a poor prospect for apples— —

Tom is just telling us from the Courier of Sir Humphrey's presentation to the Prince Regent— I am disappointed that the Even[g] is wet as I had hoped to see something of Hereford— we must be off early in the Mor[g]. if the Weather suits— or, we shall not be in time for Piersford[6] on Tuesday— I shall write to morrow & send another letter off to thee on Tuesday or Wednesday— I suppose if we go on as Tom expects we shall reach home on Friday when the first thing I look for will be a letter from thee— Tom & Joanna beg thee best love I ride J.M.[s][7] Mare J Mrs Urwick's Poney I was the stouter traveller farewell M. W.

Mem. We returned from this proposed journey— to meet a letter bringing the acc[t]. of the death of our dear Child Catharine, which was followed by her Father. What a blow to our happiness. Our first sorrow which had overtaken our married life— My Companion in his Fathers absence darling Tho[s] was taken from us in the Dec[r]. of the same year 1812   M W

[4]Mary wrote "if."
[5]Mary wrote "if."
[6]Piercefield.
[7]John Monkhouse.

24

William to Mary, 30 May 1812

Despite his impatience with London society and its ill effects on his health, William found congenial pleasures in city life and was anxious to make a good impression. The cost of his new town clothes suggests that he did not wish to be mistaken for a tasteless rustic.

At Charles Lamb's, William read *The Waggoner* aloud. He wrote this comic poem in 1806, and when he published it in 1819 he dedicated it to Lamb. *Peter Bell*, written in 1798, frequently revised and also published in 1819, William dedicated to Southey. William enjoyed reading his poetry to an audience and from all reports read superbly, in a resonant, manly voice, with a strong north-country accent—"like the crust on wine," Hazlitt avowed. The Lambs' visitor, Martin Charles Burney, was the nephew of Fanny Burney, the novelist.

Although its population edged above a million in the 1811 census, the London William walked was but a slim fraction of the sprawling metropolis it became during Victorian expansion. Still separated from the city by pastures and meadows, Hampstead remained a rural village, sought out for its health-giving waters and restorative air. The plan John Nash designed for Regent's Park was published in 1812 but not laid out until 1814.

Thomas William Carr was solicitor to the Excise. History has concealed what disaster occurred in the kitchen when he visited William and Dorothy at Dove Cottage.

William Wyndham, Baron Grenville, and Charles Grey, the second Earl Grey, had previously held powerful cabinet positions. After Perceval's death, Lord Wellesley and later Lord Moira negotiated unsuccessfully with Grenville and Grey to form a coalition ministry. They did not hold cabinet posts in the new administration.

Elton Hamond, an idealistic young man of letters, wrote a great deal without surrendering his manuscripts to printers. He killed himself on New Year's Eve, 1820, and was thought to have been insane. Now known as Kenwood, Caen House, near Hamond's home, was the seat of William Murray, third Earl of Mansfield and Caen Wood. Maria Edgeworth, the Irish novelist, enjoyed considerable popularity in England during the Regency. The lawyer who accompanied William and Henry Crabb Robinson home from Hamond's was J. F. Pollock.

The guests at Lord Mulgrave's dinner party not previously introduced included Augustus Phipps, commissioner of excise stamps, taxes, and inland revenue, and his wife, Maria Thellusson Phipps, a serious amateur artist; Sir Abraham Hume, collector and patron of the arts; Francis Basset, Baron de Dunstanville of Tehidy and Baron Basset of Stratton, statesman, scholar, and philanthropist; Benjamin West, the American historical painter, who had settled in London and was president of the Royal Academy; and Charles Long (later Baron Farnborough), paymaster general and another patron of the arts, whose wife, Amelia, was Hume's daughter. The Countess of Wellington, Catherine Pakenham Wellesley, was the wife of Arthur Wellesley, Earl (later Duke) of Wellington and general of the British army. Wellington's numerous infidelities won him the nickname the Beau.

William enclosed the sheet that he had omitted from his last letter as the beginning of the letter following. Counting the two sides of that sheet as pages 1 and 2, he numbered the first page of his new letter "3." He parenthetically provided some instructions for locating contiguous pages, as the pattern he followed in writing on the versos of his sheets was erratic.

Saturday morning

Dearest Mary

I send you the conclusion of my last Letter. — I rose this morning at 7 to write to thee my beloved. Yesterday, I walked from the Lecture with the Morgans and dined and supped with them by previous invitation. On returning home I found a Letter from thee with the Enclosure from Sara both of which I read before I went to bed with infinite pleasure. How unlucky that you now wish to start on Tuesday, as you will not be able to receive this Letter; nor can hear from me at all now for a week or ten days. I had provided a frank for to day calculating that it would reach Hindwell on Monday which would be six days after you set off on your Tour and perhaps two days before your return; but then to welcome you on your return, I had provided another frank for Monday, to be received by my Darling on Wednesday; and all this pretty arrangement is rendered fruitless; so that my Letters will lose 3 4^{ths} of their value by being put into your hands, like a *bundle* of old newspapers. Where as had you set off at[1] the fixed time there was one provided to greet you on your return, if your Tour had lasted *less* than a week; and another if a day more. Well my sweet Love will regard this as a mark of my Ardor & ever loving thoughts of her. Oh my Mary! my own Darling, one thought one wish, one longing for thee such as now pervades my Soul & every particle of my Frame, turns human existence with all its cares & fears into a heaven of heavens. I am as a Husband, and a Father, and a Brother, the blessedest of men! —

I am now writing before breakfast, because this day I go to Hampstead to dine with Miss Baillie, and she requested that I would be with her early to take a walk before dinner. Accordingly I purpose to call on Coleridge about 12, and part of the time after breakfast (we begin breakfast about a quarter past nine) I shall have to spend with the Beaumont's.— But now let me tell thee that I do not go to Coleorton; joyful knowledge for me as it will be happy news for thee. In fact the B's are not likely to be there before six week's, perhaps two months are gone; so I am wholly relieved & *handsomely* released from that obligation; and therefore at liberty to be so much sooner with thee, to take so much the earlier a flight into thy blessed arms. — Ten days at the *utmost* will, I hope, suffice, for Bocking and for Mrs Clarkson; and within a month of this day I hope to have a kiss from thy lips, and to see Hindwell and you all. But

---

[1]William wrote "&."

then come the Wheelwrights surely they will not interfere with us. after this piece of good news let me tell thee that thy missing Letter has reached me; the Gentleman, by the bye those Gentlemen ought never to be trusted with letters between Friends that love as we do nor with any Letters of importance) the Gentleman must no doubt have forgotten his Charge. Furthermore; I find that I did thee wrong in the formal enumeration made in my last of thy Letters; I have since discovered that I omitted one & considerably the longest; and for this omission I beg pardon.— I thought in truth that there was another in existence, and sought for it carefully, but as I keep my Letters among my Linen, I had overlooked this one, which had contrived to slip itself into the folds of a shirt. By the Bye did I tell thee that I have been obliged to lay out a deal of money in clothes, a new black suit, £6.15, a Hat 28s. a pair of silk stockings with cotton tops & c 9— and I am afraid they will scarcely prove worth the money. I was obliged to pay half a crown for having my hair cut, and the price of the hat is very high, being bought in this neighbourhood but the Man guaranteed [it] to be a good one, and my other is as brown as if it had been worn ten years.— But to return to Letters; none now are missing but the long one intended by Dorothy for us both.— I am glad of this— I think Sharp's Clerk must have neglected to put it into the twopenny off.[2]— Next Wednesday I shall see him & will enquire.

Now let me continue my story, from the point where it ends in the half sheet which ought to have gone yesterday week, viz Friday. That day I dined with C.[3] & the Morgans, and before ten hurried off to Lamb's where I read the Waggoner, to L— his Sister, and young Burney, a nephew of the celebrated Miss Burney. If time had allowed I should have read Peter Bell in preference. I am pleased to say that they were all extremely gratified; and sorry am I to add that constant engagements since have not permitted me to see them; though I believe that Lamb has been out of Town, otherwise he would have been at Morgans last night. I do not remember how I spent last Satur-

[2]The office for mail to be delivered within London.
[3]Coleridge.

day Morning but in the evening I called upon Jonsy who was delighted to see me; and yet I am not sure but that here I am making a mistake; nay I believe I surely am mistaken, and it was the Wednesday preceding that I called on Jonsy of which I have already given you an account. — —

Well from Sunday I have a distinct recollection of things,— & will give you a slight sketch. On that morn at[4] eleven H. Robinson[5] & I left the stones of London Streets at eleven & proceeded through the fields, and through the intended Prince Regents Park at Mary bone, & over Primrose Hill to Hampstead. It was a cloudy morning with a cool January breeze, and we had a most refreshing and agreeable walk, on our way to the Churchyard of Hampstead a Q^r of an hour before the people came out of church. We amused ourselves in reading the Epitaphs; waiting till the Congregation appeared, among whom I did not doubt that I should find Miss Baillie, who had requested me to call upon her having learned from me at dinner at Sothebys in the course of the preceding week that I should dine at Hampstead on that day. The situation of Hampstead Church is quite pleasing, looking from among and over trees towards & far beyond the great City. Miss Baillie appeared, and we walked with her to her House; and upon entering there whom should I meet but my old Acquaintance Mr Carr formerly a Lawyer & now holding a high situation in the Excise; and honorable at Grasmere, on account of the very bad dinner which he had the misfortune of receiving, or rather dearest Dorothy and I had the vexation of giving him in our Little Cottage at Grasmere, before you & I, my Love were married. With Miss Baillie & this Gentleman we conversed nearly an hour upon politics and alarmed each other not a little by the mutual communication of thoughts & observations. —

Carr is [a] very respectable Man whose office & connections give him an opportunity of seeing much; and his report is in some respects, especially as far as relates to the Country encouraging. But the state of parties among the upper classes, and the want of principle, and above all of a decisive char-

---

[4] William wrote "&."
[5] Henry Crabb Robinson.

The Prince Regent, later George IV, by Sir Thomas Lawrence, c. 1814–15. The National Portrait Gallery, London.

acter, in the Prince Regent, not to speak of other deficiencies in him, still more to be deplored, these endanger every thing.
— The Prince's conduct is described to be capricious & unprincipled in the extreme; and he does not appear to have the slightest strain of common human feelings. Before you receive this Letter you will have learned from other sources who are to be Ministers. It is now confidently talked that the Grenvilles & Greys (plague take this one to come in!) with that profligate Man Lord Wellesley, & Canning.[6]—
From Miss B's we walked with Carr to see his house & family.
— He is most charmingly situated, a House, which though not many yards from the public road sees nothing of it, but looks down the hillside sprinkled with trees over a scenicly rich woody Country, like one of our uncut forests, towards the smoke of London and upon the Kentish & Surrey hills far beyond. "Green rise the Kentish Hills in chearful air.". This said I is a sweet Spot, Yes answered he and I have reason to love it with gratitude for I believe it saved my Life. He then told me that in consequence of severe application to business his health had entirely failed, a complaint having been generated the seat of which he thought was in his heart, and I came here, said he, as I believed to die.— But relaxation from business & pure air, by little & little restored me, and I am now excellently well & my children 8 in number healthy & flourishing. The seat of his disease proved to be the Liver; he is now quite well (Look for page 8) and blooming but in the lines of his face are traces rather of sickness than years. When I last saw him about ten years ago he was the most youthful & healthful looking Man of my acquaintance. From his House we went to Mr Hammond's— H. R's Friend with whom we were to dine. He is a young Man, occupying with his Sister a pleasant Cottage on the top of Hampstead Hill, the front windows looking Northwards towards & beyond, the Spire of Harrow on the Hill, and the back windows looking down a little wild slack or dell towards & far beyond the Metropolis. And on the left in

[6]Words omitted.

the same view stretch the extensive woods of Lord Mansfield around Caen House. This Mr Hammond has had the moderation to withdraw nearly though not I believe entirely from business, preferring leisure & retirement with a little Literature, to heaping up money amidst care & anxiety. He is a young Man of elegant & somewhat feminine appearance, much attached to rural scenery, and having paid some attention to poetry & works of Imagination. But in these things he has much to learn; I attempted to let a little light into his mind, and perhaps some things said by me may here after produce some change in his opinions. He is a passionate admirer of Miss Edgeworth & knows a good deal of her family, having resided some time among them in Ireland. Of Miss Edgeworth I spoke a I thought; mentioning at the same time that I had read but few of [her] works. — He bore my observations with great good temper and upon the whole I liked the man, though I think his mind wants strength.

We had a pleasant walk home in the evening; and I should have been much improved in health by this day, but that imprudently instead of turning quietly into the House, whither H. R. accompanied along with a Lawyer who had been of the Party, I must needs, finding the B's[7] not a[t] home, take a turn with them towards their quarters. And sure it is that this additional Hours walking did my stomach and head considerable harm; but how so ever the case, I have no prudence in managing myself. But here let me say that though my stomach is weakened and it feels over burthened, and though I perspire a good deal in the night from heat & hurry in the day & from the very late dinners, with more wine than does me good, yet still upon the whole my health is improved and for these last ten days I have had scarcely any thing of my old enemy; and this I ascribe much to my having been spared in sleep, and in the mornings I am always as you would wish to know that I am. I never shall forget the sweet demonstration you gave me at Liverpool, when I was unwell, that I was far better than I was willing to believe. Tell me if you have ever thought of that since we parted.—

[7] Beaumonts.

On Monday I dined with the B's at Lord Mulgrave's, present Mr and Mrs Phipp's, a Sir Abraham Hume, Lord Dunstanville, a most friendly and agreeable noble man) Mr West the Painter Mr Wilkie, and Mr & Mrs Charles Long, (look for page 10) of the treasury. This Man Long was the person who prevented Luff having the place[8] of Paymaster which Lord C. Somerset designed for him. His Wife draws ably and is supposed to have many fine accomplishments; I did not like either the one or the other of them. I sate by Mr West the Painter, and had a very interesting account of the first determination of his mind to the art of Painting, which I shall have much pleasure in repeating to you. One anecdote I will here mention. The first thing which he can remember of his performance in the art was as follows. It happened that an Aunt of his was staying with his Mother (by the bye I ought to mention that Wests parents were Quakers, & he lived and was brought up among Quakers exclusively) this Aunt had a little child with her and one day his mother going with her sister into the garden to gather flowers, left the child[9] in its cradle sleeping under little Wests Care, with a charge that he should fan away the flies from its face. Having undertaken this employment West observed upon a desk near him an inkstand with bottles of black & red ink, & pens & paper. Instead of continuing his enforced labour he turned to them & proceed[ed] to attempt a Delineation of the infant slumbering beside him. When he had made considerable progress in this effort his Mother & Aunt returned with their flowers, Espying them & fearing to be scolded for neglect of the Child he huddled up the paper, but his Mother insisted upon seeing it, she gained her wish & exclaimed this is little Jane, upon which she snatched young West up in her arms and eagerly kissed him. "And that kiss, said the old Painter now 75 years of age, that kiss did the business."— Well Mother if thee be so pleased with the picture of the Child I'll draw for thee the flowers also."— He then told several other particulars of the growth of his passion for the art & his education for the practice of it, which I reserve for our meeting. —

[8]William wrote "placed."
[9]William wrote "children."

When we went up stairs at Lord M's I found the Countess of Wellington, the Wife or rather Widow bewitched of Lord Wellington the General. — She is next to the daughter of Dr Darwin[10]— whom I mentioned some time ago the most engaging Woman I have seen in London, very pretty, even handsome, and of an intelligent expression, but all will not suffice to fix [   ] [de]bauchee her husband, who has licentiou[sly connn]ected himself with a succession of other [   ] O miserable life— oh high blessing of true [   ] virtuous love! What rapture is one soft smile from the heart (or rather from the soul), or a kiss from a lip of the wife & mother, even if time have somewhat impaired the freshness of her virgin beauties; what higher rapture is the consciousness that even for the pleasures of sense, the soul is triumphant through the might of sincere love, over the body; and that the mind can spread over the faded lips a more than youthful attraction, and preserve for the frame of the Beloved one an undying spirit of delight & tenderness, which the soul feels in itself, and can impart with confidence & certainty to that human being which is the Lord of its affections. O My Mary such happiness has been, & 'heaven be praised') yet is ours.

Take care of thyself my love, and above all of thy eyes and give me good accounts of thy progress towards health & strength. As I have another frank for Monday and as this cannot be read till probably 8 or ten days are gone, I will pause here. farewell my darling, love me more than I deserve to be loved; and think of me as often as it makes thee happy to think of me & dost thee good, but no more, & no oftener. Love to every body not forgetting Miss Monkhouse. I was much pleased with the account of dear John and will contrive to bring some thing for him. — If I thought it possible that this Letter could be received by thee before my next I should add something to it. But to morrow you must depart on account of Piercefield. again & again farewell

W. W.

[10]Mrs. Maling.

25

William to Mary, 1 June 1812

William began his letter with tender reflections, but in resuming his journal of events he seems to have borrowed a nib from the pen of James Gillray, the satirical artist who so bitingly caricatured contemporary life in his mordant cartoons. In William's sketch, Samuel Rogers' scarcely human guests obsessively pursue their favorite vices. Uvedal Price, portrayed as a dissipated glutton, had won public notice for his books on the picturesque landscape. Lady Caroline Carpenter Price was his wife; Miss Price and her brother, their children. Foxley, the Price estate in Herefordshire, is twenty miles from Hindwell, and William had passed a day and a half there in August 1810.

Sir Harford Jones (later Brydges), diplomat and author, retired from the East India Company after returning in 1811 from an appointment as envoy extraordinary and minister plenipotentiary to the court of Persia. Joseph Jekyll, member of Parliament for Calne, was better known for his wit than for his political insight or expertise. Richard Fitzpatrick, gouty bon vivant and member of Parliament for Bedfordshire, died in 1813. Thomas Hampden-Trevor, second Viscount Hampden, was the heir of the seventeenth-century patriot John Hampden, who defended the rights of Parliament against the tyranny of King Charles I in the English Civil War.

At Lady Crewe's rout William met the princess regent, Caroline Amelia Elizabeth of Brunswick-Wolfenbüttel, wife of the prince regent. Their marriage had been arranged by the prince's father, and within a year of the wedding the prince forsook Caroline to live apart.

In his interview with Lord Lonsdale, William amplified the points of the briefer appeal he had made by letter in February.

The relative he mentioned at Appleby was a Mr. Wilkin. Southey sought Lord Lonsdale's patronage at this time as Louis Dutens, historiographer royal, had died in London on 23 May. Although he failed to receive this royal post, Southey was appointed poet laureate in 1813, when Walter Scott refused the honor.

Dr. Matthew Baillie, Joanna's brother, was a distinguished anatomist; he had married Sophia Denman. Miss Baillie remembered little Dora from a call she had paid the Wordworths in Grasmere in 1808.

Mond June 1st. Eleven in the morning
Last night my sweet Darling on my return from Hampstead I was greeted by the Enclosed from Dorothy and a delightful Letter from thee dated May 23^d. I cannot explain how these Letters have come so irregularly. I have had one of May 25th in my possession two or three days; and in the instance before a Letter which was sent off some days before another did not come till several days after it. Never mind since they have come at last and I have at this moment lying on the table before me 8 of thy most dear Letters besides the one of Sara to Joanna, giving so interesting an account of our Son John.—

On Saturday, I sent thee a long Letter, which thou wilt receive at the same time as this; I wish this could have been otherwise.— I came in last night wet and read both the Letters in bed. Thine was the tenderest & fondest of all I have yet received from thee, and my longing to have thee in my arms was so great, and the feelings of my heart so delicious, that my whole frame was over powered with Love & longing, Well was it for me that I was stretched upon my bed, for I think I could scarcely have stood upon my feet for excess of happiness & depth of affection. I lay awake a long time longer than I have ever done except the first night since I came to London, partly from over exertion in the course of the day, and still more

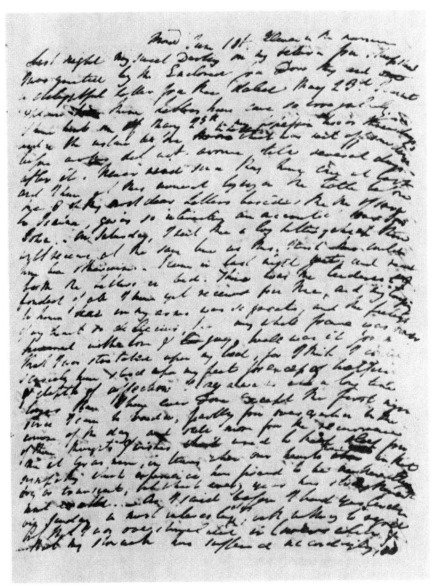

The first page of William's letter to Mary, 1 June 1812 (Letter 25). The Dove Cottage Trust, Grasmere.

from the recurrence of those thoughts & wishes which used to keep sleep from me at Grasmere, in times when our hearts were in that sympathy which experience has found to be neither illusory or transient, but which every year has strengthened and exalted.—

As I said before I had yesterday viz Sunday a most interesting day, with nothing to regret but that I was over stimulated in Conversation & that my stomach has suffered accordingly, so that at this moment I can scarcely keep my hand from it.— But I will resume my journal— On Monday as my last Letter will have informed you I dined at Lord Mulgraves. And on Tuesday at Rogers's, present the B's[1] Mr Price Lady Caroline, Miss Price and her Brother; with whom I talked about Hindwell. He complained of his Companion Sir Harford Jones, an orientalist, who took no interest in farming, and who interfered much with his wishes to see some of the Management. Accordingly I ventured to invite him to ride over during my intended stay in Radnorshire; he is [a] very well looking & agreeable Young Man. Nothing could be more deplorable than the rest of the Party: Miss P— a little deformed Creature, with a most strange enunciation, sitting by Mr Jekyll a celebrated Wit, and quite pert and to use a coarse word ever rampant upon him. She is, as Sir G. observed in expression of countenance & manner just like the bad Sister who does all the Mischief in a Faery tale. Lady Caroline was coquetting away with General Fitzpatrick her old Paramour, who is a most melancholy object, with a complection as yellow as a frog, a tall emaciated Figure & hobbling with the gout. He creeps abroad yet, poor Man, and may fairly be said to have one foot in the grave. It was lamentable also to see poor Price overgorging himself at dinner as he did, and falling into a lethargic sleep immediately after, from which he had not power to preserve himself two minutes together. This was truly a piteous sight for Price is a man of genuine talents, and gifted by Nature with a firm Constitution which he is destroying by gluttony. He invited me to Foxley, and if you could ride so far I should be glad to go with

[1] Beaumonts.

you to shew you the place. — Jekyll I believe I mentioned before; he is a man of exquisite conversational powers but did not shine on that day, not having the needful quantity of wine, which Rogers forgot to push about. Lord Hampden was of the party also an elderly man of the first fashion, but interesting to me only because he possesses the Estates of the great patriot of that name, and by the female line— is of the same family. —

On Wednesday The B^s had a party at home to dinner, but it was not very interesting, several of the invited having sent excuses, being engaged with the present occupations which the slate of parties has created. Mr Lister however was there. He is the eldest Son of Lord Ribblesdale, and if he survives his Father will be proprietor of Gowborough Park, and Malham Tarn &c. The former place Sara & I visited with much pleasure last summer; and the Latter is famous for fine fishing. I had a good deal of talk with him; and he said that he should be happy to shew me a glen near Malham & Gordale, wholly unknown to Travellers, with which he was sure I should be highly delighted. In the evening came in Lady Lonsdale, two of her daughters, & the Lord himself, with a Star upon his breast and the Garter round his Knee. — As several Persons were in the room besides, I had no conversation with him. I left a card as probably I told you some days ago, and this morning have written a Note requesting an interview for a few minutes. —

As to Politics the old opposition seem confident they shall come in, but nothing is yet decided. It is clear the Prince Regent is most averse to them: but I fear they will be forced upon him. In fact the country is in a deplorable state; and if firmness be not shewn by the government, with descretion also, disturbances wide & frightful are inevitable. The Prince is neither respected nor love[d] by any class of Men. By the bye I forgot to mention that from Lord Mulgraves we went to Lady Crewes, and there I had the honour of being introduced to the Princess Regent; an empty honour, for her R. H— was at some distance from me, and I had no conversation with her. She is a fat unwieldy Woman, but has rather a handsome & pleasing Countenance, with an expression of hilarity that is not however free from Coarseness. This was a large Assembly, saw few pretty

Caroline of Brunswick, consort of the Prince Regent, later Queen Caroline, by
Sir Thomas Lawrence, 1804. The National Portrait Gallery, London.

women, and many most disgusting objects; one I encountered
of a tolerable face & features, but in her native bosom so huge
& tremendous, that had you seen her enter a room in that condition I am sure the soul of modest womanhood in you would
have shrunk almost as with horror. Her Breasts were like two
great hay-cocks or rather hay stacks, protruding themselves
upon the Spectator, and yet no body seemed to notice them—

But to come to something more interesting. It now wants
only 20 minutes of four. Just as was concluding the last page I
received a Message from Lord Lonsdale in answer to my note
that he would be glad to see me at 12. I posted away immediately. He shook me by the hand and received me very
kindly. I began with enquiries after his Family, then thanked
him for his Letter, and for Giving me this opportunity of
seeing him.— I beg[ged] leave to state in addition to the un-
favorable circumstances in my course of life, mentioned in my
first Letter, that had appeared to me to justify the representation I had made to him, was to be reckoned a calamity which
had befallen our family in the person of my Brother Captain
Wordsworth, who, he would recollect, had lost his life by Ship-
wreck. I said that My Brother had entirely sympathized with
my literary pursuits, and encouraged me to give myself entirely
to that way of Life, with assurance that [if] I stood in need of
assistance, and he proved fortunate, it should ever be ready for
me. — I requested also permission to supply what appeared to
me deficient in my second Letter—, deficient I mean in the
expression; I had thrown myself in the mere form of words
more upon his Lordships recollection of me, I said, than[2] I had
a right to do. I wished to give him no unnecessary trouble, and
if I could procure knowledge of any thing that was likely to suit
me I certainly should not be so wanting to my own interests as
to omit making an immediate application. Of course all this was
soon cleared. I then said that by way of giving him a general
Idea of what might suit me I would mention the place of Dis-
tributer of Stamps, now holden by a Relative of mine at Ap-

[2]William wrote "that."

plebye; I had endeavoured to learn the emolument of it, but could not speak accurately, but I thought that place should it prove vacant would suit me, — but I adverted to it merely as a General guide for his Lordship in this service to be done to me. He then said, that I must be aware that all his influence of this kind depended upon the Government which was now in an unsettled state. To which I replied that I was sorry for the condition of the Country in this respect; but I hope such arrangements would be made, as would not exclude his Lordship from that influence which his family and character entitled him to. — He then very amicably entered into conversation on indifferent topics for at least twenty minutes, chiefly relating to Persons & things in Cumberland & Westmoreland; he leading the Conversation; and when I took my leave he shook me by the hand; and said "I shall not be unmindful of you": — Tell me if you are satisfied with this. I am, & know not what more I could have done. His Lordship told me that he had this morning received a Letter from Mr Southey, requesting his exertion to procure him a place recently vacant by the Death of a Frenchman of the Name of Dutens. It is that of Historiographer to the King, or some thing of that kind.

Having given[3] you a detail of this interview, every thing else will appear insipid. I will only add that On Thursday last I had a most pleasant day with Rogers & Sir G— at Greenwich where we walked about that Glorious Park; & I could not help thinking how happy we could have all been there. The East Indiamen were returning from an unusually short & successful voyage, three ascending the River full sail, and one of them, I believe the Ship (though I did not then know it) the unfortunate Abergavenny's Successor. I had melancholy thoughts of poor John,[4] but upon the whole it was a most pleasant & rememberable day. On Friday C—s[5] Lecture, dined and passed the evening at Morgans. I like the two Women[6] much & will tell you more about them; some other time. On Saturday called at

[3]William wrote "giving."
[4]William's dead brother.
[5]Coleridge.
[6]Mrs. Morgan and Miss Brent.

Coleridge's by 12 & he walked with me as far as Hampstead; we did not part till half past three; I dined with Sergeant Rough at Miss Baillie's; the wife of Dr Baillie, and a party in the evening, a pleasant day; slept at Mr Carrs, and the history of Sunday yester day would be very long; it was a most agreeable day but I was exceedingly exahusted by long talking. Sir Humphrey & Lady Davy dined with us; I sate by Joanna Baillie, and had a long chat with her. Among other topics were discussed our little Dorothy who had charmed her much and Walter Scotts wife, with whom to my utter astonishment she had been much pleased. This brought out my feelings with regard to the Lady luckily Davy was there; and he supported what I spoke to her prejudice. I did not scruple also to say that you & Dorothy & in fact all of us had received the disagreeable impression. Miss B— said she had seen her in her own House, that she appeared to admire her Husband was attentive to her Guests, had her House apparent[ly] well ordered, & her children under excellent management. Besides, said Miss B— she wore a bunch of Roses (I do [not] know if they were artificial) in front of her cap or bonnet; and I did not like her the worse for that".

But enough adieu my darling; a thousand kisses and embraces long & tender! I have another frank for the sixth of this month; ie— next Saturday; I should write sooner if I hope[d] the Letter would reach you, but if you only begin your tour it will be impossible, as you will surely be out above 8 days.

Thy faithful Husband   W.W

26

Mary to William, 2–3 June 1812

Mary's breathless effusion conveyed her exhilaration in at last beholding Tintern Abbey after her pilgrimage along the Wye. The sightseeing appeared to energize rather than fatigue her. The rude family at Usk, Mr. and Mrs. John Olive (Oliff), had lived at the Hollins in Grasmere until 1802. Jane (or Jenny) Mackereth came from an old Grasmere family and later returned to her birthplace.

William Henry West Betty, "Young Roscius," made his stage debut at eleven and bewitched his audiences as a boy actor. On one occasion Pitt adjourned the House of Commons so that members could witness Betty's Hamlet. Another time the army had to be called out to preserve order as mobs swarmed outside the theater where their idol performed. By 1812 the craze had subsided.

Mary probably added the note under the date (also underscoring the "2") when she appended her memoranda to Letters 23 and 31.

Chepstow— Beauforts Arm's Tuesday
Even^g 10 oClock June 2^d
Two days before Catharine died!

My dearest William

Having just played a good part in the destroying of a Couple of Chicken & drank a Glass of Wine I feel as fresh as if I had not stirred from my own fire side— therefore I will not go to bed another night without writing to thee my best beloved!— You must not expect me to give a detail of what I have seen— my thoughts & spirits have been too much in a tumult to suffer me to collect myself sitting as I am with Tom & Joanna talking over the same table upon which I write— I shall merely set down where we have been, & what *has best pleased* me shall be referred till our meeting— —

I forwarded my last enclosed to Mr Sharpe from Hereford on Sunday evening, we having gotten a wetting— the Rain continued violent all night— the Morning cleared while we were at breakfast (having slept comfortably) we afterwards walked about the Town & set forward at 11 oClock— the Day became very fine— with a beautifully clouded sky & a delightful 3 hours ride we had to Ross— there we saw the church & the prospects from the Meadows adjoining the Church yard &[c]—, whilst dinner was preparing— afterwards we hunted out a blind road by the *Wye-side* to Monmouth which place we reached about 8 oClock having passed a glorious afternoon— We had tea & then walked about the Town as long as we could distinguish one object from another— When we returned to the Inn— indeed my dearest Love, though I was not the least tired with my ride— my pulses were all beating & I so much enjoyed *perfect stillness* & freedom from exertion of any kind that I could not even ask for pen & ink to write to thee— at Ross I had not time as you will have observed & this Morning we were off as soon as breakfast was over— & O William what enchanting scenes have we passed through— but you know it all— only I must say longings to have you by my side have this day been painful to me beyond expression We coursed the back of the Wye all the way from Monmouth to Tintern Abbey— the River on our left hand— now *close* to us now at the distance of a stones throw— & now & then we were separated by a part of the wood which hangs over the Margin— I hope you have paced this blind track— for never did path lead amongst so much loveliness— what divine Villages! — but I must not think about them now for Joanna wants to be in bed— —

The River Wye at Tintern, showing the abbey, by Philip James de Loutherbourg, 1805. The Fitzwilliam Museum, Cambridge.

At 1/2 past 1 oClock we were seated within the Ruins of Tintern Abbey— a finer day never shone & at that hour I do not think that we could have seen the place under greater advantages— I sate a long time alone in a deep nich & I would have given the World to have had thee by my side— all these things as I said before we must talk about— We eat bread & cheese at Tintern & did not arrive at this place till after 8 oClock having drank Tea at St Arvens after we had seen the grandeur of the Wye in conjunction with the Severn & those fine rocks from Wind Crag— after Tea we walked along the Walk of Pierce-fie[l]d which I suppose you have also seen— I can only now say that all these thing[s] exceeded[1] far far exceeded my expectation— & what you will be delighted to hear I have performed my journey thus far without the least fatigue— Tomorrow we

[1]Mary wrote "exceeding."

Tintern Abbey, by Joseph Mallord William Turner, 1794. Crown copyright. The Victoria and Albert Museum, London.

proceed by Ragland Castle to Abgavenny how farther I cannot say— — the Clock strikes eleven & poor Joanna wants to be in bed— she is however much less tired than she was last night— to morrow I hope she will not have any fatigue to complain of. God bless thee I know not what I have written— but this I know, that if you could but know how much I have thought of thee today— thou woulds[t] not complain of me for having failed to bestow more time in writing Good night My Darling love— I shall not forward this till tomorrow night.—

Usk Wed. night 1/2 past 10 oClock Having satisfied ourselves at Chepstow this morning we set forward to Ragland where we dined & saw the Grand Ruins of the Castle (I hope you know this magnificent Pile that we may talk of it)— learning that Usk was only 5 miles from this place tho' it would be 6 out of our way to Abergavenny— Tom was so good as [to] accede to my wish to come this way for the sake of seeing the Olive's & Jane Mackereth— Accordingly we came— the road led us through a very pleasing Country into this beautiful Vale— we found a very pretty Town with a respectable ruined Castle— a fine one I should have said had we not just left Ragland— it was about 7 when we alighted at the three Salmons— we ordered Tea & the first thing I did was to write a Note nearly if not exactly in these words "Mrs W. of Grasmere, accompanied by the Brother & Sister, being on their way from Chepstow to Abergavenny & learning at Ragland that they were within 6 miles of Usk Mrs W. could not resist the inclination to turn aside to call upon Mr & Mrs Olive should she be so fortunate as to hear they are at home & disengaged. Should Mr & Mrs O.[2] be from home Mrs W. would be glad to see Jane Mackereth at the three Salmons— knowing that it would be a gratification to her Father & Mother to have such communication from their Daughter" This note I addressed to Mr or Mrs O. or in case of their absence to Jane Mackereth and gave it to the Waiter to send to Mr O.'s— at the distance of 1/2 a mile— the Waiter told me they had just passed to the Play (a strag-

[2]At this point Mary mistakenly inserted "not" between the lines.

gling set who have been acting in this little Town for the last 3 Months) I therefore desired the Note might be carried thither & given to Mr O. the Messenger returned with Mr Olive's Comp^{ts} and that he was sorry he could not attend!! I was thunderstruck at such a message having thought how glad they would have been to have an opportunity of hearing about Grasmere— I thought surely this must be a mistake & he will be following— but no, it was even so— & I want you to acc^t. for this if you can— could his pride be wounded that I had addressed the Servant upon the same cover as the Master & Mrs? or what could this mean? —

We ordered beds as it was now too late for A.[3] & I determined not to lose the *main* part of my errand & knowing that the Gentry were deeply engaged set out to call upon my Countrywoman— Tom at the same time went a different way to accompany Joanna upon an errand of Charity She had been much interested by a narrative which she some time ago read in a Newspaper of an old Clergyman who resides in this place & who it was stated had brought up 8 Children never having received more, from his professional duties as a Clergyman & Schoolmaster, than 13 Guineas a year— that the hardness of the times had tempted him to apply for some assistance— but this was done by means of a private letter, which the person to whom it was addressed chose to make public— —

I walked about 1/2 a mile up the Usk which is a broad & clear river with beautiful woody banks the western sky & Welsh hills in front of me & reached *the Cottage* a large square building like one of Mr Harrison's— sweetly situated— after walking a while about the grounds hanging over the River with Wood & the hidden road between (for I did not chuse to enter the house) Jenny who was not within when I asked at the door joined me & most happy & thankful was she to see me— I took her back with me to the Inn door & we talked over all the news of Grasmere— she goes in 6 weeks to be her Brother William's housekeeper in Finsbury Square— I now met with T & J. returning from their visit very much pleased— they had found

---

[3] Abergavenny.

all according to report & no doubt she had made the old Man happy for she gave him a guinea— It appeared that— he only has duty to do once a fortnight but in two separate churches— for which duty he receives ½ a Guinea a time & he teaches a few Children in his house. — All his Children except 2 are dead & of those 2, one a Young Man is[4] an Ideot— the other a Girl fit for service is obliged to stay at home to attend upon her Brother— the old Woman told Joanna that she did not *now* lament the loss of her Children as it would have been such a pain to them to have witnessed their late poverty (they could not have lived if it had not been for a Lady at Bristol who was kind to them— they did not chuse to let their parish know the extent of their poverty for the dignity of the profession)— I suppose a subscription had been made from which they have had benefit. I should have liked to have seen this pair if I had not been called another way— We have since been at the Castle & upon the Bridge & we were much delighted with what we had but a very imperfect light to see— We promise ourselves that we shall gain much by coming this round as we shall have a fine ride up the River in the Mo^{rg}— I shall dispatch this from Abergavenny— the post does not leave this place before tomorrow afternoon— God bless thee they say it is past eleven— Bless thee again & again—

12 oClock Abergavenny— after a delightful Ride up the Vale of Usk— we are most glad that chance led us this Road for Tom was quite ignorant of this being such a very beautiful Valley— he thinks it most superior to the Vale of Clwye[5] (I spell wrong I know)— so rich in Trees & woody Hills & such a very fine River! — I never saw a number of *genteel* Cottages so little disfigure any Country— indeed in many instances they greatly ornament it— We are now going out to see this old Town & Castle— whither we are to bend afterwards I do not know they seem to be divided whether we must proceed homewards by the Hay, or to Hereford, where we partly engaged to meet

[4]Mary wrote "in."
[5]Clwyd.

George tonight to see *Young Roscius* perform— I should at once decide for the Hay if we had not the other Jaunt in view when you are to be with us & when— I suppose we must go by the Hay to the Devil's Bridge— This being the case I will leave the present decision to them. At any rate I will close this letter now & if we go by the Hay, will put it into the Post here, if it is stamped Hereford you may conclude we have reached that place in safety but as we shall be late I shall not have time there to tell you so.

God bless thee. I am not the least tired— This seems to be an interesting old Town— here are a number of the French— continued fine weather

We are going to H[6] but we shall be too late for the Post or Play— 4 oClock

[6] Hereford.

27

William to Mary, 3–4 June 1812

William dropped the satiric tone of his preceding letter, modulating his voice from the irony of drawing-room comedy to the soft intimacy of the lover. Throbbing with his longing to be with Mary, this letter is probably the most eloquent and passionate that he ever wrote. Unfortunately a corner of the manuscript was burned, as Mary dolefully explained in Letter 31.

Again William quoted from his "Tintern Abbey," composed during his second walking tour of the Wye valley in 1798, on which Dorothy (addressed in the poem) had accompanied him. Lady Beaumont's sister was Anne Willes. With this letter William forwarded a letter from Dorothy, which has not survived; the information it contained regarding the welfare of Annette and Caroline was regrettably lost with it.

Wednesday aftern[oon] 2. o clock.

My dearest Mary,

Unwilling to lose a moments time I take up the pen in a place where I ought to have been long ago, viz— T. Monkhouse's Country House.— —

Thursday Noon. I wrote no farther than the two lines above before T. Monkhouse returned. I sate within above half an hour; he then walked with me to Dr Stoddarts in Doctors Commons, and was so kind as to accompany me to the door of Sergeant Roughs Bedford Row, where I dined; so that we were upon the whole together between 2 & three hours. He seems a most amiable & excellent Young Man; quite worthy of his Brother & Sister. I did not omit to give him my sentiments upon his course of future life; and he seemed fully sensible of the justice of all I said concerning his not retiring precipitately to the Country, till he had acquired a fortune considerably above his present needs; in order to guard against future demands.—

I shall pass one day with him at Hampstead; and it is not impossible that I may see him this very day, as I have just sent him a Note by the two penny Post that the rest of this present day is at my Command, and if he can take me in his Gig to Hampstead I shall be happy to attend him.—

Yesterday I breakfasted with Sharp from whom I procured this present Frank; otherwise, if you return on Friday that is to morrow, you would have had to wait till Monday you heard of me; and that would have seemed a long time, after having been so highly fed with Letters from Grasmere & from Grosvenor Square, as you have been lately. If you do not reach home till Saturday, this will make the third letter which you will find waiting for you, and as I have a frank for Saturday also, you will have another, probably however only a short Letter, on Monday. I received very expeditiously your sweet Letter from Hereford; That very evening, viz Tuesday, I had been reading at Lamb's the Tintern abbey, and repeated a 100 times to my self the passage O Sylvan Wye thou Wanderer through the woods," thinking of past times, & Dorothy, dear Dorothy, and you my Darling. The weather has been good & therefore I trust you have had a delightful Tour without any untoward accident; oh that I could have been with you. I long to be with you, I feel nightly and daily, waking & asleep the neccessity of my not prolonging our separation; and I have the happiness of saying, that I can now look forward with some confidence as to the Time.

My *residence* in London may now almost be considered as closed; for on Monday I depart with Chris^r for Bocking. He stays there a week, which time if I find it pleasant I shall pass with him; shall then move on to Mrs Clarkson, with whom I shall stay at least a week, and during the course of the third week shall find Christopher again at Bocking & perhaps may be tempted to stay with him till he returns to Town at the close of the same third week. So that on Saturday three weeks God willing I shall certainly at the latest be returned to Town, where I shall stay three or 4 days and no more, and then proceed to Worcester; where your Brother Tom will meet me in his Gig, and we will make a short excursion to Malvern Hill which I am told is very beautiful and then for Hindwell where I shall, I trust be the happiest of men— with You all & thee, my beloved.

A month!! it seems a long time to look forward! but I have wished to take in my thoughts the very utmost allowance of time I can possibly require; and perhaps I may be able to make less serve; certainly shall if I find that a week will at all satisfy Mrs Clarkson; for then instead of staying the whole third week with Christ[r] at Bocking a couple of days, in addition to the first week could be quite enough, but if Mrs C— detains me till the middle of the third week, I cannot do less than wait till the Saturday when Chris[r] must return to Town— to return along with him. So that now we see our way clearly!— and I can express the satisfaction I feel; particularly as I have discharged all claim of attention my excellent Friends here have upon me. And Lad[y] B—[1] has had the frankness to tell me, that the room I now occupy will be of use to her Sister Miss Wills; who is in a deplorable state of health, having now been several days in the House without my having seen her once, and Sir George himself as he told me, having only seen her twice. She never comes down stairs, being afraid of meeting any one; My Room is on the same floor with the one she occupies, and Lady B— has kindly told me that the range of both rooms perhaps would be amusing & therefore might be of some use to her. — This communication which I obtained to day decided me; otherwise

[1] Beaumont.

I might perhaps though not very probably put off my journey a few days. — So that every thing is most lucky. — How I long, (again must I say) to be with thee; every hour of absence now is a grievous loss, because we have been parted sufficiently to feel how profoundly in soul & body we love each other; and to be taught what a sublime treasure we possess in each others love. — I am happy to say that my health has been much better, and could I manage myself as to exertion, I should be strong & well, for every cause but one; which injures me, though upon the whole I never was before so well, or had so little to complain of in that respect. But I feel every day & hour that herein I shall fare worse, the fever of thought & longing & affection & desire is strengthening in me, and I am sure will be beginning to make me wakeful and to consume me. Last night I *suffered*; and this morning I tremble with sensations that almost overpower me. I think of you by the waters & under the shades of the Wye, and the visions of nature & the music of [   ] raptures of love, the love I felt for thee [   ] not venture to *tell* what he felt [   ] which inspired me as an honoured & cherished [   ] and lastly as a [   ] as an expecting Bride [   ] Husband seated for ever on the [   ] as a Father, and a long tried sharer of [   ] pleasures; — each and all of these [   ] existence have passed through my mind, [   ] over again my past self, & thy past self also, [?participating] every sentiment of thy heart & being, as far as Nature would allow what thou hast been, from the hour of our first walks near Penrith till our last parting at Chester, and till thy wanderings upon Wye, & till this very moment when I am writing, & Thou most probably art thinking of me and losing all sense of the motion of the horse that bears thee, in the tenderness & strength of thy conceptions and wishes, & remembrances. Oh my beloved— but I ought not to trust myself to this senseless & visible sheet of paper; speak for me to thyself, find the evidence of what is passing within me in *thy* heart, in thy mind, in thy steps as they touch the green grass, in thy limbs as they are stretched upon the soft earth; in thy own involuntary sighs & ejaculations, in the trembling of thy hands, in the tottering of thy knees, in the blessings which thy lips pronounce, find it in thy lips themselves, & such kisses as I often give to the empty air, and in the aching of thy bosom, and let a voice speak for me in every thing within thee & without thee. Here I stop & wherefore,— Oh what an age seems it till we shall be again together under the shade of the green trees, by the rippling of the waters, and in that hour— which thou lovest the most the silence the vacancy & the impenetrable gloom of night. Happy Chamber that has been so enriched with the sweet prayers of thy pure bosom; with what gratitude shall I behold it! Ah Mary I must turn my pen from this course.

I hope that Davy will let me have an Angling Rod, and I will take care to bring Isaac Walton.[2] As to George I know not what to say I do not yet see any means of serving him, but it does seem a pity that he should bury himself in a small farm. I think it would be best for me to write to Curwen, as I am not likely to see him here.— As soon as you receive this write to me at Bocking; and let me have at least 2 Letters during the week I am there; you will be able to make the calculations; as Chris^r returns to Town on the Saturday I shall probably leave at the same day for Bury. Now my love proceed no further with this Letter, till you have read the accompanning one

[   ] Surely you will agree with me that D— [   ] in saying that if I were to refuse [   ] Luff; it would imply a suspicion [   ] What strange reasoning: Luff is no Man [   ] of no legal knowledge, procured This [   ] in a great hurry & distraction of mind [   ] so easy as that he should have been mistaken [   ] [?mistaken], that is, if the security be no avail, [?nor] can I consistently with what I am either to myself or to him advance the money, when he has expressly told me that he would rather die than I should lose it. Observe then what I shall do; I have called several times on Woodriff & have found him either engaged or out; I purposed to call again yesterday but was unavoidably prevented; if the security prove invalid, I shall write to Luffs Father, state the

[2]That is, *The Compleat Angler.*

whole particulars, and lay Luff's Letters before him, I shall do this if Woodriff approves it, & beg that he would be security for the amount; and if he refuses and no other friend will do it I cannot see that either weighing Luffs feelings & situation, or looking at my own *I ought* to do it. You have read the affecting Letter from Caroline & Mother; how can I be justified in throwing away or running the risk of throwing away so large a portion of our little property as 100£, those claims existing against me added to those of thee & thine. There can be nothing honourable in a conduct so opposite to the clearest dictates of nature & justice. And as to Sara— that is an after consideration— Tell me what you think of this Account from Annette & Caroline. T— Monkhouse can get Letters sent for me into France, and I have therefore given one to him for that effect. Does not Annette appear to have behaved well (& even in a dignified manner; I shall be happy if it appears so to you—

My darling you will be quite lost amid this length & magnitude of Letters that will encounter you on your return— You will have to³ lock yourself an hour & a half in your own room before you have travelled through them it will [be] a journey, as far as relates to name, like that you have just made through the miry and rough & difficult ways of herefordshire. I have scarcely reperused a page of my Letters to you, and therefore I know that in addition to the illegible penmanship you must have had to encounter⁴ the puzzling effects of innumerable omissions of words, commissions without number of wrong words making utter nonsense. But your ingenuity and patience will I hope suffice to put all to rights

It is now half past one Thursday, and I am not without a fluttering hope that every knock at the door may bring me a Letter from you, and yet this is foolish for you probably would not be able to send off a Letter on Tuesday, and if so I must moderate my wishes. God bless you I hope all is going on well with you; that your Horse does not stumble, and that it will not

³William wrote "to have too."
⁴William wrote "encountered."

take fright. Being in the City yesterday I called on Mr Clarkson, saw him only for a couple of minutes for he was at dinner, he looks as well as usual. As soon as I have finished this half sheet, I shall write a short note to Mrs Clarkson, telling her when she may expect me, I have owed her a Letter for more than a week; but she is indulgent. indeed if she knew what a length of time I have employed in writing to you & in Letters almost as long to Grasmere, she would not be inclined to find fault with any appearance of neglect to herself. —

I should have had more time if I could have risen regularly by half past six or seven; but I have lately dined out a[lmos]t constantly & seldom sate down till aft[er] [   ] that my nights have been feverish from so [?late] a [   ] which acts like a heavy supper; and bein[g] [   ] from other causes I have not slept so well having heated myself in walking too much at night in the streets; for example, last night I walked from near Grays Inn (viz. Mr Rough's House) with Christopher & H. Robinson to Lambeth Palace, thence to Grosvenor Square & thence to the end of Oxford street and back again, which was too much; but I got to talking with H. R— and was not sensible how tired & heated I was. We had a pleasant day at Roughs and I read the Waggoner with which they seemed much pleased. The first part hung rather heavy, but nothing else appeared to answer amiss. Rough is a very good natured Man; his Wife had not yet come down stairs from her lying in but Christ[r] and I as married men were admitted into her apartment where we sate half an hour. There was present also a Pupil of Roughs who seemed to enjoy the poem much. I have seen nothing lately of the Montagu's— and shall not see much more of Coleridge— but he dines here to morrow with Sergeant Rough & Christ[r]. He dined also here on Tuesday with Joanna Baillie. He does not talk of Keswick & Grasmere. — I shall leave this slip with a chance of a letter arriving from you or from Grasmere, before it will be necessary to seal my frank— if it does thou[5] not consider this as a farewell.

W W.

[5] Word omitted.

[*232*]

I have been obliged to tear off part of D's Letter on account of the frank— the paper I have written on is very heavy.

I cannot bid thee adieu on the other side, farewell, with a fervent kiss my beloved wife

W. W.

28

William to Mary, 6 June 1812

As William announced in his first sentence, this letter is uncharacteristically short. The Robisons were friends of the Hutchinson family; Mary referred to Miss Robison as her oldest acquaintance. William Mackereth, brother of Jane Mackereth, was probably the Mackereth on whom William called with Tom Monkhouse.

Saturday morning. June 6th

My sweetest Mary,

This will be a very short Letter. — I ought to have provided myself with a couple of quires of very thin & light paper, when I first came to London; for I have found several times that I have overloaded my franks, & if sent in that state we should have lost as much by one of those, as we have saved by three or 4. Yesterday, on this account I was obliged to send a Letter to Grasmere in a very garbled state.— To day you are returned or probably will return from your, I trust, fortunate & pleasant excursion. — I have a frank for Monday, the day I go to Bocking you may therefore expect another short Letter from me by your Wednesdays post.— but to continue my Journal.

On Wednesday afternoon T. Monkhouse took me up with his Gig and carried me to Hampstead. Where I sate three hours with Mr & Mrs & Miss Robson¹ & T. M— and then by

¹Robison.

previous engagement drank tea with Miss Baillie; returned about 11 & supped with the Robsons where I slept. Next morning returned to the City with T. M— Called in passing on one of the Mackereths, T. M— stated to me that he was under great obligation in his business to Robson which he had no present means or prospect of future means of discharging. He added that Robson was of the Fish-Mongers' Company the wealthiest & most respectable of London; that the Court which governs this company consisted of about 30 Members, who had very considerable patronage &c &c, and that he was sure it would be very gratifying[2] to Robson to be in the way of becoming a Member. Now your Friend, Richard Sharp said T. M. is Warden or chief officer of this company, and if he would at your request take Robson by the hand, it would probably bring about in course of time his appointment; and I should then in some degree repay the great obligation I am under to him. I replied that I would take up the business immediately; accordingly I called on Sharp yesterday, stated the Case, he allowed me to bring T. M— to him, and told him what he could and would do to promote the object; and Robson is to call upon Sharp in the course of the week: This business took me up the whole of yester morning At 3 I attended Coleridges lecture, hurried home and he Chris^r Sergeant Rough & myself dined with the Beaumonts. This morning I am going to have an interview with Mont: and Woodriff about Luffs Money; which has been a heavy restraint & plague to me. — T. M— advises me also to make a Copy of the Letter to be sent to France,[3] & send the Duplicate by another conveyance. This will be an hours work; and I assure you in writing such long Letters to Grasmere as well as to you I have employed many a long & let me say happy hour, farewell my darling. it grieves me to send so short a Letter—

[2]William wrote "gratified."
[3]Written above "Annette," which was deleted.

29

Mary to William, 6 June 1812

Mary described her return to Hindwell and the banquet of letters that awaited her as one still overwhelmed by such a profusion of cheerful news and affection. She remained ignorant that the day before her excursion ended, little Catharine had died in Grasmere. Mary's tender solicitude for William's French daughter seems especially poignant in this context. As a dowry William paid Caroline £30 annually after her marriage in 1816, until in 1835 he settled a sum of £400 upon her.

Saturday Afternoon June 6th.

My dearest Love

We reached Hereford from Abergavenny on Thursday (where I put my last letter into the post) after somewhat of a weary ride; for after the first few miles the road was uninteresting & we were obliged to ride the whole way, 24 miles, without baiting there being no resting place on the road— I think I never passed so thinly inhabited a country— we got *in* about 1/2 past 9 oClock went soon to bed & were quite fit to start again in the Morning— We came home by Weobly— a village that looks beautiful with its spires in the Valley particularly after you have passed it in connection with 2 curious little round high hills the Piorn[1] hills— the most remarkable things

[1] Pyon.

upon this road is Mr Pepton's fine House & a peep (which was to me very interesting) into Mr Price's recess² far distant— —

We were a good deal fatigued with the heat of this day tho' we rested a good while at Weobly— we reached home at 7 oClock— I washed myself had tea & was greeted by the sight of thy letters & never after felt that I had been on horseback— 2 large *packages* from thee! the one sent last, by the bye, that which contained D˸ long letter was charged 3/4!!— never mind it was well worth it— I devoured these as long as I could see & then was obliged to lay them aside a while till after supper when I shared part of my pleasure with the rest, by reading parts from them— this kept us up till after eleven— when in my own room I feasted myself again, but this did me no good for it was day light before I got to sleep & then we rise here again about 7— however I am now as well as ever I was in my life— tho' my spirits are somewhat humid— for at dinner thy last dear pacquet reached me & it is so deeply affecting a letter that I cannot attempt to reply to it— the whole of the Morning I spent after *re*perusing thy former letters in writing to Grasmere which I was obliged to do somewhat at length, not having written since the day before we expected to set off upon our tour, and were disappointed— In this last letter you beg me to write immediately— therefore I could not be at rest without doing so, or I should have done more justice to my feelings had I waited till tomorrow— as it is I must write briefly & get things of[f] my mind.

In the first place I am glad that the time of your departure from London is so near at hand— & satisfied in my own mind that I have some guide when to expect you— but the space between seems far more distant than I expected it to be from some of your former letters— it is a very long time— a whole month yet, & I now have been 2 months here! what an age will it be till we see our Darlings at Grasmere— yet the time will seem very short when you get to me! — But do make all the haste you can. I know you will I need not desire it— I do indeed think Annette's conduct very dignified & most heartily

²Foxley.

wish we were rich enough for you to settle something handsome upon dear Caroline— perhaps if any thing good comes of your application— we may— I was much pleased indeed with your exertions in that affair & think what was said was sufficiently hopeful— but I wish it may come soon— I do not mean any particular thing. With respect to Luff's business I gave you my sentiments before— I do not look at it exactly in that point of view that they do at Grasmere so far as this, that is, if they mean to say (as you interpret the words) that your refusal would imply a suspicion of Luffs integrity— I do not think *that*, nor can I think they meant any thing more than— — Yes I have looked again at[3] the letter & this *is* what they mean— I do not agree in this, but I think your refusal *having made the promise* would shew a want of confidence in him which would not agree with the sort of friendship you have shown for him— & I think the loss (should it prove a loss) would be *even to us* so small that I would risk it rather than have the pain of thinking that you had wounded the feelings of a *poor Man who* has the highest respect for you— I certainly *should advance the* Money & apply to no one further for security. —

Dear little Tom was glad to see me back— but he is excessively fond of his godmother[4] & she of him— he has been quite good about his book & she wishes to have the teaching of him herself— One thing I forgot to tell you that the Morning I went away he started up out of his sleep & said "Where's *my* father? is my father come?—" the next moment he was collected & his dream for dream it had been was passed away— he says he must not stay— he must go to *his sweet Willy*— he does passionately love his little Brother. I dare say Tom will be very glad to attend you to Malvern Hills— but he will be kept busy having to attend a summons from Mr Clarke to meet him at Shrewsbury in the course of this Month— The Wheelwrights will be here they expect in about a week— about the 19th. Miss Weir will be here— the W^s will be gone we think before she reaches us— so you see we shall have a full h[ouse] however

[3]Mary wrote "&."
[4]Mary Monkhouse.

nothing of this will interfere [w]ith our happiness— I do think it would [be] well to write to Mr Curwen— perhaps something may be done in Essex or Suffolk—

I exult in the thought of another letter from you so soon— I shall be more collected & write at length in 2 or 3 days— at present I must leave off having scarcely seen the face of any one of the family except at meals to day It was a great satisfaction to me to read to them what you say of Tom Monkhouse I hope you may see him again— if you cannot call upon him only send him a line & appoint where he may meet you & he would be right glad of the pleasure he said once or twice in his letters if he only knew where to find you he would have called upon you— He means to be at Penrith in the autumn you must ask him to Grasmere to see Mary[3]— My kindest Love to Chris: & his family & to dear Mrs C.[6] I am not sorry that her husband is from home. Dear Caroline & Annette I cannot help recurring to them again the account they give of themselves is very affecting— & creditable to the Mother— She must be a nice Girl— but I should hope that her time is not so completely shut out from all exercise & pleasure in life, except what they find in each other as D. represents from the letters— a Woman like A— I think must have found some connections that would lead them somewhat out of themselves & in that case, however strict the attention that is required for their office may be; they might relieve each other & refresh themselves by change of scene— constantly in that place for one so young as C is terrible to think of! but I hope this account may not be accurately translated— D. does not say how she expresses herself that is whether she writes french well or not— God bless her I should love her dearly & divide my last with her were it needful— God bless them both & thee my best beloved my soul & every nerve is full of thee

[farewe]ll M.W.

[3]Mary Monkhouse.
[6]Catherine Clarkson.

William to Mary, 7–8 June 1812

William finished his last letter to Mary the morning before he departed for Bocking with his brother Christopher. The manuscript is fragmentary, concluding mid-sentence with no hint of a farewell. How many pages were lost or destroyed cannot be determined.

Miss Hindson, sister of the elder Mrs. Addison, had been the bridesmaid at the wedding of William's parents in 1766.

William appears to have been heartened by Coleridge's more regulated habits while in residence with the Morgans. The *Friend* was the periodical that Coleridge produced with the loyal assistance of Sara Hutchinson during his sojourn at Allan Bank. Twenty-seven issues were printed between 1 June 1809 and 15 March 1810. In 1812 Coleridge talked of resuming publication, and the collected earlier issues were to be offered for sale at 18 shillings. The original price was a shilling per issue, but subscribers' payments had been haphazard.

The *Tatler*, a periodical launched by Richard Steele, also carried contributions by Joseph Addison; it ran from April 1709 to January 1711.

Sunday 2 o clock

My dearest Love,

I have been occupied nearly three hours this Morning in making a Duplicate of a Long letter of Dorothy to France and of my own. T. Monkhouse who will forward these Letters by the means of Merchants of his acquaintance who have licenses advised me so to do as not one Letter in three reaches its destination; I have also called on the Davies, and Sir H— is to send me a fishing Rod to Grosvenor Square, which I shall bring down with me to Hindwell. I called also on the Ladies Fleming but did not find them at home; I called there also yester day morning; so that I have done my duty here. — To morrow I depart for Bocking at 3 o clock in the afternoon— so that the morning is all which remains for me to settle the business with Montagu and Woodriff. — I called yesterday on Mrs M— who affects and *perhaps* feels great kindness towards you but says nothing of Dorothy & Sara. — I should have written you a Long Letter this morning; but you have been told how my time has been occupied, nothing can be conceived more tedious than copying french, especially when like mine & poor D's also it is not good—-

Now let me tell you my Sweet Love, that on returning home last night I was gree[te]d by your fondly expected Letter with Abergavenny Post Mark. How happy am I that you have been delighted & that you stand the fatigues so well. I knew that if the weather favored you would be charmed with the Country; but I was very apprehensive that the fatigue would injure you; and your health is above every thing precious to me. — The Olives are worthless creatures without any heart. These last words explain why they did not trouble themselves to see you, you measured their enthusiasm by your own sweet nature; further as you mentioned your B^r & Sister they were probably afraid that you should accept the Beds which they must have felt themselves bound to make you an offer of. Next; they probably thought it very hard to pay their money for the play, and not have their penn'orths. I am sorry very sorry that the stupid Roscius led you back to Hereford; and could earnestly have wished that instead you had gone up the Usk as far as Brecon, and then returned by the Hay. I have twice been up the Usk and a charming country it is; this really mortifies me; I paced this tract once alone on foot, and great part of it in the same way with Dorothy and C.[1] You cannot think how much dearer

[1] Coleridge.

the Wye is to me since you have seen it; I loved it deeply before on most tender remembrances & considerations but now that you have seen it also & know it, & we [?now] can talk of it together what a sanctity will it attain in my mind, and of all my Poems The one [in] which I speak of it will be the most beloved by me. —

Here I was interrupted; it is now eight Monday Morning. I have been up an hour, washing, dressing, putting my things in order for my journey to day &c &c— I shall leave my trunk till my return, & take as few things as possible. — I am quite puzzled how to act on my return to London; the Beaumonts will be going or gone;— I do not like to quarrel with Mrs Mont: nor can I bring my mind to give her such a public testimony of regard as would be implied by putting myself under her roof— therefore I am as yet quite undecided where I shall be during the week I purpose to spend in town on my return. — You cannot conceive also what a trouble I have had & time I have lost in this affair of Luffs too, I have at least made ten calls about it; nor have I yet brought it to an issue. This morning I shall have to betake myself to it again. It was a most unwarrantable application on Luffs part; and on every account I do exceedingly regret that it was ever made. —

Yesterday (it is now Monday morning observe) Coleridge was to have called on me by appointment at eleven to walk in the Park. — Soon after came that good Creature Morgan with an apology that he was ill in bed— in fact he had been (2nd slip of paper) quacking, and brought on the pain in his bowels.[2]— I employed the morning in writing, and between two and three called on the Addisons whom I found at dinner, Mrs A— Miss Hindson Mr and Mrs Rich^d A— and a young Lady I suppose Miss A— I sate, I think an hour with them, & then called on C—[3]. I found Mrs Morg:[4] at home, & C— appeared shortly. Mrs M— I think, I once described as a handsome woman, but

[2]My parentheses; quacking: treating oneself, playing the quack doctor.
[3]Coleridge.
[4]Morgan.

she is not so— She has a round face, dark eyes, an upturned or a pug nose, nevertheless as her complection is good, her eyes bright, and her countenance animated & goodnatured and she has the appearance of being in redundant health, she is, what would be called, a desireable woman; neither too fat nor too lean; but just what, in that 1 respect, I and your other friends would wish you dearest Mary to be. The other Sister has a smaller round face, an upturned nose also, and is thinner & more delicate in appearance and of more still & gentle manners; not that there is any thing unpleasan[t] in Mrs M— on this score; but Mrs M's carriage [   ] person is more [?unwary] luxuriant & joyous.— I fear [   ] with all these words I give you no distinct Idea of [   ]. I sate there about an hour. Coleridge upon the whole is much better in health, & appears to live far more rationally than he did with us, so that he has changed for the better assuredly; and I think his present situation & employments upon the whole quite eligible for him.

Tell me frankly, can you decypher the scrawls I send you. I am never so happy as when writing to you, what a pity that my penmanship is not better. — Lady Davy has engaged to give me 4.4 for three subscriptions of the Friend; so that, by little & little, some are picked up. — Coleridge proposed to come down for a couple of days to Bocking, and if we can manage it, we are to cross the Country to Chatham to see Captn Pasley for a day and a half, I know not how far this will be practicable. He seemed to enjoy himself so much, and the Country air & objects appeared to do him so much good, the day he walked with me to Hampstead, that on this account I shall be happy as far as depends on myself to give effect to his proposal. — So that upon the whole there appears small likelihood of my leaving Town till comes a month dating from last friday afternoon, for on a Friday afternoon I certainly take my departure with T. M.[5]— —

Examine upon the Maps if you are able how Oxford lies in respect to Hindwell as to distance &c— Thomas[6] & I settled

[5]Tom Monkhouse.
[6]Tom Hutchinson.

[243]

that he was to meet me at Worcester, but if by leaving out Worcester he, by the addition of thirty miles or so, could meet T. M.— at Oxford it would be a high treat to us both, and T. might see Oxford & Blenheim two of the finest things in their several ways in the world. Do mention this. How much my darling, do I regret that when we returned to Coleorton we did not make a deviation to include these. Observe what I mean it is forty miles, if I mistake not, from Hindwell to Worcester, now if by the nearest road, Oxford should prove to be no more than 70, would it not be worth T's while to make a push for the sake of seeing it. — I ask this with difference, but it would be a pleasant thing if practicable. —

You will risk no extravagance but this very moment I have parted with no less than 20 shillings thus. a 5 & sixpence piece to the person who has made my bed while here, another to him who has cleaned my shoes &c and three 3 shilling pieces to Sir Georges' Servant, for his personal attendance upon me. Is this too much? or would less have sufficed? I purchased on Saturday the Tatler, unbound a neat Copy for 4.6 This is surely very reasonable, and we do not possess the Book. I could buy many works which we want reasonably[7] had I the money. — Coleridge says that he shall soon be clear of all his embarrassments, and that he finds fagging pleasant to him. — Certainly he is quite punctual as to his Lectures— How gladly could I scribble away

[7] William wrote "reasonable."

Mary to William, 8–10 June 1812

In her final letter Mary entered another late annotation under the date. Her exclamation "Our Child had been 4 days dead!" suggests the wondering disbelief she must have suffered in rereading the lines hopefully anticipating Catharine's "progress towards perfect restoration." Unsuspecting, she wrote the words when Catharine already lay in her grave.

Devereux is unidentified. Miss Weir had to be paid for Dora's school fees at Appleby, and Mary realized that the income from the Stockton farm she had recently inherited would probably be consumed by legacy duty. The servant Sarah Youdell had been ill with debilitating fevers throughout the late spring.

William's "account of poor Charles Lamb" must have stood in the concluding section of his last letter, which has not survived. Lamb, however, is known to have overimbibed on other occasions and embarrassed his more temperate friends with his bonhomie.

This letter was forwarded from the Deanery at Bocking to Wordsworth at Hindwell.

Monday Afternoon June 8th — 3 oClock
Our Child had been 4 days dead!

My Dearest William

Joanna & I walked to the post & met with your letter according to my expectation this morning— I cannot express how greatly I admire, & how deeply I feel thy goodness in having thus perseveringly sent off one long letter after another— I am indeed almost *sorry* that so much has been demanded from you— I am sure you must have been harrassed, sometimes, by the thoughts of procuring franks, & *having* procured them in attending to their date— not to speak of the *time* that so much writing required— God bless thee! for my part I shall be everlastingly obliged to thee & I know that thou feelest thyself repaid by the assurance which thou hast in thine own heart, how great the joy has been, which thou hast bestowed upon me. —

Thou art now upon the road to Bocking, if not already arrived there, I am very glad that you have turned your back upon the great City— the quiet of Bocking & Bury I hope will be a cordial to you after all the hurry & bustle you have been in— so many calls you have had upon your time— so many unpleasant duties to perform! indeed my Love I have not been unmindful of these things— I have admired & *worshiped thee* almost when I have observed the industrious zeal with which you have gone through each & all of these— Having finished with Woodriff, whom I am sorry to see you have not yet done with— you may finally quit London with triumphant self-satisfaction & oh that the time were here, when *perfect* repose shouldst be thine. —

William that dearest & sweetest of all thy letters, which affected me so much on Saturday when I received it that I could not trust myself to speak in reply to it— that dear letter as I was reading it over in bed before I slept— last night (as I had done the preceeding one) caught fire, & the corner was burnt off where thou hadst so feelingly traced the progress of that affection which in different situations thou hast felt towards me— I was sor[ry to pa]rt with the *written* assurance— but dearest William the remembrance, which is [   ] repetition of what thy tongue has uttered in the tenderest moments,— that I have seen the words impressed by thy hand out of the bustle of the noisy world when I was far from thee, never will pass away— —

Thy short letter of this morning was quite as much as I expected— & indeed my Treasure thou hadst no need to make me any apologies for I do wonder how you have found leisure for so much writing— having as you say sent nearly as long letters to Grasmere as those I have been blessed with! I was most glad that you had it in your power to oblige T.M.[1]— it was most kind in you to set about the Work immediately— Mary read me a letter from him to day, in which he speaks of the exertion you so readily made for him, with great delight; & I am sure you have seen no one since you went to London who has had more *real, heart*felt gratification from your society than T.M.— & glad I am that you have seen him— In his letter he presses my B[r]. Tom to meet you at Oxford instead of Worcester— but poor Tom will have had too much, to come into this plan without some more important reason than he has given— for he set off again upon a long journey yesterday at 4 oClock— at 2 he rec[d]. a summons from Mr Clarke, or rather a letter for Tom to appoint to meet him either at Shrewsbury or some other place, if he could not make it convenient to go forward to his house at Ellesmere where he would rather wish to see him— however this said letter had been so long upon the road that Tom had no choice left— there was no time for an answer to be sent but He was obliged to hurry off immediately in order to catch Mr C at his own house before he quitted it, either upon this day or tomorrow, for Stockton— This is sharp work for Tom— only having been at home one day before he was taken away again— I suppose we cannot see him before Wednesday Evening again at the soonest. J.M.[2] & George are gone to a fair to day at the Hay.

I am now writing by my open window (after 8 oClock) having been looking at a Gentleman fishing upon the pool which is quite alive— the fish are plunging on all sides of him— It is Mr Whitaker who lives at Knill Court— he has been here several Evenings lately— his Wife & Daughter who drove up to the door in their Carriage are now walking by the side of the pool— the Lady will not condescend to walk in— he is an eager sportsman kept his Daughter upon the Water with him till near

[1] Tom Monkhouse.
[2] John Monkhouse.

10 oClock the other night— I am sorry to hear the bad acc[t]. of poor Miss Wills— her situation must have greatly damped Lady Beaumonts pleasure— which she otherwise must have had in your society—

Dearest William what nice thoughts thou hast about our seeing all thou talkest of together but this can never be; but never mind we shall be happy enough without it— It would be far too expensive— how could we go but on horseback— & how could such horses be procured— traveling homewards— The tour we have already made has not cost less than £15— I calculated upon an average £3 a day— You will think this almost incredible— but take along with you, that we were in an expensive part of the Country & Tom for sake of the Horses always chuses the best Inns— & those will have the highest price— I should hope the Devils Bridge excursion will be a less expensive one— however dear Tom does not mind it— he deserves plenty for he has no niggardly spirit about him. —

Wed: I was interrupted here on Monday Eve[g]— Yesterday Morning I busied myself in making Tom a pair of Trowsers, & we had Company to dinner, so as I did not mean to send this letter off before to day, I was not anxious to finish it till I had received thy last letter from London previous to your departure for B.[3] & this mor[g]. it was brought to me in bed— You must know that the post which brings your letters arrives at Radnor at 11 at night & we usually fetch them the next mor[g]— but this mor[g] they were sent— The weather is changed it is much colder & it is beginning to rain. — I trust your absence will not be prolonged *beyond* the Month specified, I almost fear it, when you talk of having so much to do—

By the bye T.M. having mentioned the idea of my Brother Tom meeting you at Oxford I shall not repeat it, unless I am so determined from seeing an inclination in Tom when he hears the proposal— because I cannot think it would be convenient to him, he having been so much from home & having yet to take *me* a long journey— The Horse that goes in the Gig is

[3]Bocking.

used at the plough & in a fortnight from this time it must be taken off to fetch Miss W.[4] from Shrewsbury which no doubt would be a reason against Tom wishing to detain it so [soon ag]ain as would be necessary to meet you at Oxford— knowing the situation of things it [w]ould be indelicate in me to make the proposal & I am sure you will see it in the same light that I do—

I am very glad that you have got your dispatches sent to france— have you supplied the Money to young Devereux— & written to his friend? — It is an awkward thing that you cannot return to your old lodgings in London— as it is not accordant to your feelings to go to Montagu's— & certainly I should avoid staying there if you think *M.* has behaved dishonorably towards you— as to *her*! I should be sorry that he should suffer for her sake— I have not yet heard the particulars of what passed between C[5] & you on your reconciliation— therefore am no judge how far, that is, *how much farther* M. is reprehensible than when you went to London— in the darkness which I am in— the case to me seeming to rest upon the word of one & the word of the other— I should be at a loss to fix upon which of the two I ought to depend. — I have no doubt however your own feelings will direct you right in this particular— When you saw R[d]. Addison did he tell you that he had a small parcel for you to bring to Hindwell— he took a silver Mustard pot to be mended which you are to bring back so if you please you must continue to ask for it. — Be sure you do not come in a *shabby coat* or hat & I could wish you to bring at least 2 Changes of linen— for George has come ill provided & if you have not your own things with you likewise, it might perhaps cause more washing here than would be convenient as we shall be such a very large family— I have told you this *now*, it being upon my mind in consequence of your speaking about putting up your things & perhaps I should have forgotten it at a more seasonable time— —

I cannot think you have been too lavish in your gifts to the

[4] Sarah Weir.
[5] Coleridge.

Servants you could not have done less. God bless thee I have nothing to blame thee for. I want some money sadly & I grieve to name it to thee thou hast had so many calls upon thee— I can do without till you come but you must come well supplied for our journey— I fear we shall have no 1/2 years rent to receive in Aug: from Stockton, which was the source whence I meant to draw Miss Weir's pay for D.,[6] for Sarah[7] tells me she has had a deduction of £33 for Legacy duty & when our rent-day arrives there will be the same black account given to us, no doubt— — Surely a mine will be springing for us before long.

Art thou not my Darling delighted with the accounts of dear little Catharine how I do long to see her & *that sweet Willy* as Tom calls him— D.[8] says two or 3 damp days causes a return of her lameness, it is therefore evident that our situation must retard her progress towards perfect restoration. — I am quite well & have not felt any bad effect from my journey, but quite the contrary in every respect except that, as was the case after my journey hither, my eyes have been particularly weak— after reading all the letters that I met with on my return & writing the many following they were very weak & painful— I avoid using them as much as I can— but it makes me a little uneasy to think that what gives me such exquisite delight should be the worst thing for them. — I was very much affected with Dorothy's account of poor Sarah[9]— & am glad she is not to return at the busiest time of the year as would have been the case had she come back to make Hay— I hope she may be able to return to us at Martinmas if we stay at G.[10] in which case the Cows *must not* be kept in that House— it is enough to destroy the best constitution in the world & I should think myself wicked to persist in requiring any one to attend to them there— I trust your health my beloved continues to be better & that you

---

[6] Dora Wordsworth.
[7] Sara Hutchinson.
[8] Dorothy Wordsworth.
[9] Sarah Youdell.
[10] Grasmere.

very much enjoy Bocking & your brother's Company— well should I love to be with thee in thy travels— dear Mrs Clarkson! I shall particularly long to be with thee by her quiet Couch— give my very best love to her & tell her that I bear up the hope of sometime or other being her visitor— I think it would be rather hard were I to remain the only one of us who have not had that gratification— Does she talk of coming to the North this year? —

I was very sorry when I read your account of poor Charles Lamb. what a pity he should not exercise more self-denial— it grieves me for his Sister's sake as well as his own— C.[11] & he must be most unfit Companions for each other— Dear D.[12] how she distresses herself about C's inattention to them. I wish she would not suffer such things to disturb her so much. — — No parliament formed yet! it is quite painful to me to think of this suspension— it is plain there is no one competent to be placed at the head of affairs or this could not be— all here wish *you* were the chosen one & then they are sure things would go right— for my part worlds should not tempt me to consent to your being in a situation of so much danger or of your being subject to so much anxiety— No my darling let us have our own dear retirement— with a little more money for the sake of more ease, & ability to enjoy the pleasures we derive from a little travelling the short time that it remains to be a pleasure to us— but if this cannot be, if we are only to be blessed with life & each others society &— health & power to make our Children what we would wish to be— we shall be happy— But how miserable should I be to see thee subject to irritation envy & ever in danger from thy situation to tempt the hand of the Murderer. O William— but it is folly to think of such a thing— it was the excess of my love for thee led me to muster the thought—

Little Totts is chattering under the window he is helping his Godmother to water the Garden, the rain seems to be gone off for the present— The Wheelwrights are to be here at the end

[11]Coleridge.
[12]Dorothy Wordsworth.

[*251*]

of the week— **the party** consists of Mr[13] & Mrs W. 2 Children &
a servant— **a comfort**able addition to a large family! but they
will but **sleep 2 nights** here— I have written so ill that you will
scarcely be **able to** make it intelligible— I am badly supplied
with both **pen & ink** & was loth to spend any time in providing
myself with better wanting to have my letter in readiness for an
opportunity to send it to the post— not having to go for letters
to day it is of some consequence to spare a journey. I have
always been able to read your letters with very little difficulty—
therefore write without apprehension on this account—

I am very sorry that we did not return from Usk in the way
you mention— certainly had we known that it would have been
worth while we should have done so— But T. did not know
exactly how we might meet with accommodations for the
Horses on a road he had not travelled that made him doubtful,
more especially as we had a borrowed Horse— & as I was to go
by the Hay on our next tour it seemed to me to be of less
consequence at this time— — & another thing the Horses'
backs were becoming tender & the hot weather aggravated this
evil which made us less anxious to prolong our journey— Yet
all this would not have weighed if we had had a certainty of
being repayed for our trouble— We were ill off not having
provided ourselves with a good Map— the only one we could
see at Usk was of no use— If we had had a traveller like you
with us we should have done better— but Tom is too shy to
make himself acquainted with a Country he is a stranger in, in
any other way than by his *own observations*— he is clever so far,
but he can not being himself to talk— or ask Questions of Strangers— & I am too much of the same disposition— however we
had a most delightful excursion notwithstanding the very very
great want I had of thee— how I did long for thee at all times
& how much happiness do I promise myself from what I have
yet to see when thou art by my side— May heaven eternally
bless thee & send thee to me in health & strength & with spirits
to enjoy what I so earnestly look forward to—

[13] Mary wrote "Mrs."

M M.[14] has just told me that one of the Servants is going to Kington & I must close my letter— Adieu I shall write again for a letter to meet you at Bury about Monday— Your next may guide me about the time of forwarding mine   thy M. Wordsworth

[14] Mary Monkhouse.

Epilogue

Here a chapter in the biography of William and Mary Words-worth ends. The letters stop, and we are suddenly thrust from the intimacy we shared with "the family of love," as their friends called them. The travels of William and Mary were cut short in June 1812 by the heartbreaking news of the death in Grasmere of their little daughter Catharine, who was buried in the churchyard across the road from their home before word could reach her parents that anything was amiss.

An hour after William's departure from Grosvenor Square on Monday, 8 June—the day of Catharine's funeral—Dorothy's brief letter arrived, but it failed to catch up with him in Bocking until Wednesday afternoon:

My dearest Brother—
  Sara and John & William and I are all in perfect health— but poor Catharine died this morning at 1/4 past 5 o'clock. She had been even better & more chearful than usual all yesterday— & we had fondly flattered ourselves for three or four days— in particularly noticing how much her lameness was abated, & how well she used her hand. Mr Scambler has promised us to write to you by this same post, with an account of her illness— I shall therefore say no more than that she began to be convulsed at a little before 10 last night; & died this morning at 1/4 past 5— — — Upon most mature deliberation we have concluded it best not to write to Mary— It would be impossible for her to be here at the Funeral; & we think that she will be better able to stand the shock when it is communicated by you,— You will be by her side to impart all the consolation which can be given. May God bless & support you both— We are as well as we can be after so sudden a shock— &

are greatly comforted in the Belief that all that *could* be done to save her *was* done— Yours evermore

D Wordsworth

June 4th Thursday afternoon—

If you leave London in the Ludlow Mail any evening you will arrive at Ludlow the following Evening at the same hour. (Sara believes at 8 oclock). You are then 19 miles from Hindwell by the Wigmore Lingen & Presteign Road— If you hire a horse at Ludlow it can go back from Hindwell the next day. If you take a Chaise you will go by Knighton, which is some miles further. Thus, Sara says, is the most expeditious way. There is a Coach to Kington but it is slow— Sara knows nothing about the Kington Coach but Tom Monkhouse or R^d. Addison perhaps can tell you.

We purpose burying the beloved Girl on Monday. This we do for the best— & we hope you will both be satisfied. If we had attempted to keep her till you & her Mother could come, you would not have been able to look upon her face, she would then be so changed— & it will be a calmer sorrow to visit her Grave— — Mr Scambler has been all that we could desire in such a melancholy case, & we both felt the most perfect reliance on his judgment.

Sara will write to Tom to reach him about the time that she will reckon upon your arrival in Wales; to inform you how we go on— Fear not, we shall bear up under it all— — Pray write to tell us how you are, & what you determine upon doing.— [DCP]

On Thursday morning William returned to London, packed his trunk, and hastily paid a melancholy round of farewell calls. On Friday he set off on the Hereford coach, finally reaching Hindwell on Sunday, 14 June.

From London, William had written to Tom Hutchinson, begging him to impart the sorrowful news of the child's death to Mary, but the plea was unnecessary. Mary had been present when Tom received a letter from Sara Hutchinson, carefully timed to follow William's calculated arrival but preceding him owing to his delayed receipt of Dorothy's note. Sara, Dorothy, and Richard Scambler, the physician, wrote to William and Mary at length, documenting with agonizing precision the details of Catharine's seizure and struggle in convulsions.[1] Death, Sara reminded the grieving parents, had released Catharine from further sorrow and suffering, for had she survived she could never have regained the full use of her limbs and her understanding would most likely have been impaired. Recovery from her unexpected loss came slowly for Mary, and before the restoration of her strength or mettle another blow fell on the mournful household. Six months after Catharine's death, little Thomas was laid in the grave at her side, where the children had formerly played by the river, under the shelter of a haw-thorn tree.

Some literary critics have argued that the grief of these be-reavements transformed the Wordsworths' marriage, under-mining their sense of blessedness and destroying their passion. But that is another chapter. Ours is the joyful hymn in celebra-tion of a marriage—harmoniously recorded in the worn manu-scripts that Wordsworth fervently hoped would "be preserved whatever else we lose."

[1] These letters are among the new papers now in the collection at the Words-worth Library at Dove Cottage.

Index

[*259*]

THE LOVE LETTERS OF

William and Mary Wordsworth

Designed by Richard E. Rosenbaum.
Composed by Eastern Graphics
in 10 point Baskerville, 2 points leaded,
with display lines in Baskerville.
Printed offset by Thomson/Shore, Inc.
on Warren's Olde Style, 60 pound basis.
Bound by John H. Dekker & Sons, Inc.
in Joanna book cloth and
stamped in Kurz-Hastings foil.

Library of Congress Cataloging in Publication Data

Wordsworth, William, 1770–1850.
The love letters of William and Mary Wordsworth.

Includes index.
1. Wordsworth, William, 1770–1850—Correspondence. 2. Wordsworth,
Mary. 3. Poets, English—19th century—Correspondence. 4. Wives—
England—Correspondence. 5. Love-letters. I. Wordsworth, Mary, 1770–
1859. II. Darlington, Beth. III. Title
PR5881.A483   821'.7 [B]   81-67177
ISBN 0-8014-1261-7   AACR2

Printed in the United States
137198LV00001B/42/P